Foreword

In life, we are often consumed by what is visible—the challenges we face, the ambitions we pursue, and the daily routines that demand our attention. Yet, true power often lies beneath the surface, unseen yet profoundly present within us. Reflecting on this, I am reminded of Antoine de Saint-Exupéry's words from The Little Prince: "What is essential is invisible to the eye."

mARIa Gregory's The Lion You Don't See explores this profound truth, inviting us to look beyond the obvious and delve into the depths of our inner selves. She encourages us to recognize the quiet, often-overlooked forces shaping our lives—the groanings of the Spirit praying within us, the unspoken language of our soul that expresses itself in hopes, joys, frustrations, fears, and trust. It is in these groanings, this unarticulated yearning of the Spirit, that we find the essence of our humanity and the divine potential within us.

Have you ever marveled at how you instinctively know where to place your hand to scratch an itch or guide food to your mouth without consciously thinking about it? This remarkable ability, called proprioception, is a hidden sense within us—one we use every day but rarely acknowledge. Similarly, there is an inner "lion" within each of us: a force that remains quiet and unseen, waiting for the right moment to roar into action.

This lion is real. It is the strength we draw upon when life demands more than we believe we can give, the courage we summon in the face of fear, the love that moves us to forgive the unforgivable, and the grace that sustains us in moments of despair. It is the quiet power of the Spirit at work in us, inviting us to name and verbalize the unspoken—to find the language for what we feel and to embrace even the discomforts that come with being human.

As human beings created in the image and likeness of God (Gen 1:26), we carry within us a divine essence—a "God-DNA" that empowers us to grow, mature, and embrace our full potential. This divine imprint is not distant or abstract; it is alive within us, guiding us even through the uncomfortable and unspoken moments of life. It is alright to feel, to wrestle with what is difficult, and to find our own language to express what we are going through. In doing so, we align ourselves with the Spirit's gentle yet powerful work in our lives.

Too often, when overwhelmed, we look outward for solutions, turning to external sources for strength and forgetting the lion within us. Yet, the greatest battles are not fought in the open but in the quiet, sacred chambers of our hearts. It is there that the Spirit groans, urging us to confront our fears, to recognize our pain, and to transform it into growth. This book is a call to awaken that inner strength, to trust in the divine force woven into our very being—a force greater than anything we face externally.

What you hold in your hands is more than a book. It is a guide to courage and resilience, a companion for those standing at the threshold of something great, and a reminder that the unseen parts of our soul are often the most powerful. Maria Gregory has skillfully woven a tapestry of wisdom, storytelling, and spiritual awakening that will resonate deeply with anyone who has felt the quiet call to step into their true power.

As you journey through these pages, may you discover the lion within you. May you uncover the quiet strength that lives in your spirit, learn to name and embrace your deepest feelings, and find new depths of courage and grace. And may you walk away with a renewed sense of purpose, knowing that you are never alone—your lion walks with you, every step of the way.

Fr. Gerard Jonas, OCSO
Mepkin Abbey
Moncks Corner, SC

I first crossed paths with Maria's team more than two decades ago when we were pioneering a school in one of our mission areas in the Philippines. Christian schools play a vital role in shaping children to become the hope of a better tomorrow. That was the driving force behind my work in that place all those years ago.

Though Maria and I met virtually, and despite her being abroad, we shared a common vision. I was deeply immersed in our shared goal, and she quickly became the main instigator of turning this aspiration into reality. Her unwavering love for the Lord opened doors for us to accomplish many projects that serve the greater good, especially for children. With Maria's efforts, we reached many places in the Philippines, providing aid and support when our country needed it most.

Her team extended job opportunities, provided financial assistance for education through sponsorships, and supported gift-giving and feeding programs for underprivileged children. We also launched campaigns for the youth, teaching them the value of life and how to treasure it. Every project we completed carried a story of hope and transformation.

Maria's life has been a blessing to everyone she encounters. Whether offering wise counsel or providing practical assistance, she goes to great lengths to understand the heart of any issue and offer meaningful solutions.

As I read "The Lion You Don't See," I am struck by how deeply it reflects the struggles young people face today—struggles that are often left unspoken, misunderstood, or out of their control. Maria's background in guidance counseling shines through in the interactions between Logan and Ari. Ari's attentive listening and unwavering presence guide Logan toward making wise decisions, offering a powerful model for how we can approach the daily battles young people face.

This book will be a valuable resource not only for teenagers and young adults but also for parents, helping them understand and support their children. There are many unspoken thoughts and emotions that only in silence we can begin to comprehend. The lessons woven into these pages are often overlooked in the rush of real life, but paying attention to these subtle struggles could make all the difference in connecting with our loved ones.

Jinky Enrique
Educator/Mentor
Manila, Philippines

When you meet Maria, she will always see the best in you and help you make the most of yourself. Her life reflects the presence of Almighty God all around us, and she encourages us to seek His guidance in everything we do.

Many of our troubles come from saying yes when we should have said no. We are left wondering how to handle broken people, broken relationships, broken families—and our own broken selves. Yet, it's in acknowledging this brokenness that we find the strength for new and everlasting life.

As you read Maria's "The Lion You Don't See," I hope you discover the depth of love that Jesus has for each of us. His promises remain true, no matter what we may be facing.

Happiness is a choice and a habit, rooted in our values, priorities, and attitude. What truly matters is not what's happening around us, but what's happening within us.

Maria is a wonderful believer, and her love for our Heavenly Father shines through in all that she does. Her strength comes from the joy that God brings to her life, and I know this book will reflect that same joy and hope.

Melode Rowles
Mother, Grandmother, Entrepreneur
Granville, Ohio

In today's fast-paced, technology-driven world, the simple joys of childhood are often overshadowed by the pressure to keep up. Kids are expected to excel at everything, and when they don't grasp concepts as quickly or as easily as their peers, they're made to feel left behind. The desire to be part of the "in" crowd, both in school and online, only adds to the weight on their young shoulders.

Maria Gregory has crafted a meaningful guide, not just for children but for parents too. Her words offer a comforting roadmap, helping families navigate the twists and turns of life's challenges. With her insight, Maria shows the way toward inner strength, happiness, and a deeper sense of self-worth that so many of us, young and old, are searching for today.

Michael H. Moore
US Navy Veteran, husband, father, grandfather
Oahu, Hawaii

Reading this book reminded me of the times my own family has leaned on someone like Ari. Growing up, my father often turned to his sister, whom we lovingly call Auntie. Whenever he faced a storm—whether in business, family matters, or health—she was there, offering words of encouragement, faith, and reminders of his own strength. She became his Ari, a source of comfort and a beacon of light when things felt dark. After speaking with her, he would hang up the phone with renewed joy and optimism, with a peace that only someone who reminds us of God's presence can bring.

Since my father passed, Auntie has become an Ari for me and my siblings as well. She has this unique gift: the ability to handle even the toughest situations with a calm confidence, a steady peace, and a gentle assurance that everything will be okay. She embodies the qualities that this book celebrates—a quiet resilience, a deep trust in God, and a heart that holds steady in the face of life's challenges.

This book isn't just for the young. It's a reminder for all of us that the foundation of faith, courage, and inner strength built early on will serve us throughout our lives. The lessons Logan learns are lessons we all need: that we are capable, that we are never truly alone, and that we can face anything with grace and confidence when we trust in God.

Thank you, dear reader, for choosing this journey. May The Lion You Don't See remind you of the Ari within, the calm strength we each hold that's always ready to help us navigate life's challenges. And may you, too, find someone in your life who embodies these qualities—a beacon of light in moments of darkness, a reminder that no matter how difficult things seem, there is always hope.

With much gratitude to my own Ari,

Rod Magsino
Son, Dad, Brother - Legacy Builder
San Dimas, CA

Introduction

When I created Ari, I wanted him to be more than just a companion for Logan. Ari is the mentor I wished I had as a teenager—the one who walks with you when the path is unclear, the one who reminds you that you have everything you need inside of you to face the challenges ahead.

Ari represents the courage, faith, and wisdom that we all have access to, even when we don't realize it. He is the quiet reminder that no matter how hard life gets, you are never alone. Throughout the book, Ari will be by Logan's side, helping him understand that life's challenges are part of the journey, and that even in moments of doubt, there is always hope.

My hope is that as you read this story, you'll come to see Ari as more than just a character. He's a symbol of the strength you already have within you—the strength to face your fears, embrace your future, and trust that you are exactly where you need to be.

"The thief comes only to steal and kill and destroy; I have come that they may have life, and have it to the full."
— John 10:10.

Hello, my love!

Okay, so let's be honest—life doesn't come with an instruction manual. Believe me, I've looked. And if you've ever felt like you're winging it while everyone else seems to know what they're doing, you're definitely not alone. Consider me your big sister on this journey, here to tell you: You're doing just fine.

I've been where you are—awkward moments, doubts, and that whole "trying to figure out who I am" thing. I didn't always have a lion like Ari around to remind me I was enough, but that's what I want this story to be for you. Ari's here as the voice of calm when everything feels like chaos, the reminder that you've got strength you didn't even know you had.

And here's a little secret: Ari isn't just any name. It's actually a Hebrew name that means "lion." Fitting, right? Because Ari isn't just a big, furry presence; he's the symbol of your inner strength, courage, and resilience. So, every time Ari shows up, think of him as that little (okay, maybe big) reminder that there's a lion inside of you too—one that's brave, strong, and ready to take on whatever comes your way.

This book is like a little survival guide for navigating the twists and turns of life. Think of Logan as your new buddy—he's figuring things out just like you, and yeah, he's going to make some mistakes (spoiler: we all do). But he's also got Ari, and by the end of this, I hope you'll feel like you've got your own version of Ari too—a little extra courage, some faith, and a whole lot of love.

As your honorary big sister, here's the truth: it's okay to not have all the answers. It's okay to feel like you're just trying to keep up sometimes. But don't forget—there's a lion-sized strength inside of you, just waiting to be unleashed. Life gets messy, sure, but that's where the magic happens. You'll come out stronger, every time.

So, take a deep breath, grab some snacks (big sister advice: snacks are essential), and let's dive in. I'll be right here, cheering you on as you walk alongside Logan and Ari, reminding you that you're not just enough—you're amazing.

With love, wisdom, and a whole lot of "you've got this" vibes,

Here's to your Lion,

To All Who Light the Way

Hello, parents, educators, and mentors!

Watching young people grow up and face the world isn't easy. As much as we want to be there to guide them through every challenge and protect them from life's bumps, we know we can't always shield them from what's ahead. But what we can do is walk alongside them, offering encouragement, compassion, and the reminder that they're never alone in their journey.

I understand this deeply, not only from my role as a Big Sister to Shyanne and Shantelle, whom I first met when they were just nine years old, but also as someone who believes in the power of mentorship and presence. Now, as adults with families of their own, these two incredible women are still part of my life. Even after they "graduated" from the Big Brother, Big Sister program, I've stayed connected, offering support, prayers, and a listening ear whenever they need it.

Being a mentor has taught me a profound truth: we don't always need to have all the answers. What matters most is that we're there—listening, encouraging, and showing up, especially when it's hard. As guides in their lives, whether as parents, educators, or mentors, we can't always prevent every challenge, but we can help young people find the strength within themselves to face whatever life throws their way.

That's where Ari, the lion, comes in. In The Lion You Don't See, Ari is that quiet, grounding presence we all need—a voice of wisdom and calm that reminds us of the strength we sometimes forget we have. Named after the Hebrew word for "lion," Ari embodies courage, resilience, and the fierce yet gentle strength inside each of us. He's there to reassure our kids, students, and mentees that they have everything within them to navigate their journey.

I hope this story, and Ari's guiding presence, can offer the young people in your life that same quiet support. Whether they're dealing with a difficult day at school, feeling left out, or navigating the complexities of finding their place in the world, Ari is there to remind them that they're not alone. And for all of us—parents, educators, mentors—our role is to keep showing up, offering love and encouragement, and trusting that the lessons we're instilling will help them stand strong.

So here's to you—doing your best, day in and day out, to nurture strong, compassionate, and resilient young people. It's not always easy, but you're not in this alone. I'm cheering you on, right alongside Ari.

Your fellow human,

Maria

Table of Contents

THE LION YOU DON'T SEE

CHAPTER 1

The Whisper of the Lion

Logan sat on the steps of his house, staring at the empty street in front of him. The afternoon sun was dipping lower in the sky, casting long shadows across the pavement. Everything felt heavy—school, friends, family—it was all just too much. He leaned forward, resting his elbows on his knees, trying to breathe through the weight pressing on his chest.

He didn't know how to explain it. Lately, it felt like he was walking through life alone, even when he was surrounded by people. His parents didn't seem to get it, his friends were always caught up in their own lives, and school… well, school just felt like another thing to survive. Logan wasn't sure where to turn, and for the first time, he felt lost.

As he sat there, lost in his thoughts, something caught his attention out of the corner of his eye. He glanced over to see a shadow moving at the edge of his yard. At first, he thought it might be a stray dog, but as it came closer, Logan's breath caught in his throat.

A lion.

A huge, golden lion was walking straight toward him. Its eyes, a deep amber, were locked on Logan's, and for a moment, Logan couldn't move. His heart pounded in his chest, but strangely, he didn't feel afraid. The lion didn't seem threatening—just… calm. Like it belonged there.

The lion stopped a few feet away and sat down on the grass, its tail curling lazily around its paws. Logan blinked, trying to make sense of what he was seeing.

"Am I dreaming?" he muttered to himself, half-expecting the lion to disappear.

But the lion didn't disappear. Instead, it looked at him with those deep, knowing eyes and tilted its head slightly, as if waiting for something.
"Are you real?" Logan finally asked, his voice shaky.

The lion blinked slowly, then—much to Logan's shock—it spoke.

"As real as you need me to be."

Logan jumped back, his heart racing again. "Wait, you talk?"

The lion nodded. "I do."

Logan stared at the lion, his mind racing. He had seen talking animals in movies and books, but this… this was different. This was real. "But… how? Why?"

The lion's gaze softened, and it took a step closer, its voice calm and reassuring. "I'm here because you need me, Logan. You may not understand it yet, but you've been looking for something—someone—to help you find your way."

Logan swallowed hard, still not fully grasping what was happening. "But… why me? I'm nobody special."

The lion tilted its head again, studying Logan for a moment. "You're more special than you realize. You've been searching for answers, for a guide. And now I'm here."

Logan felt his throat tighten. He hadn't told anyone how lost he'd been feeling. How overwhelmed. How much he wished he had someone to talk to—someone who could help him figure things out.

"Who… who are you?" Logan finally asked, his voice barely above a whisper.

The lion smiled, a gentle expression that made Logan feel strangely comforted. "My name is Ari. I've been with you all along, but today is the first time you're seeing me."

"Seeing you? What do you mean?"

Ari's golden eyes sparkled. "I've been with you, watching over you, waiting for the moment when you'd be ready to hear what I have to say. You're at a crossroads, Logan. You feel lost because you're trying to figure everything out on your own. But you don't have to."

Logan blinked, trying to process Ari's words. It was like the lion could see right through him, like he knew exactly what Logan had been struggling with.

"How do you know all that?" Logan asked, his voice filled with a mix of curiosity and fear.

Ari sat quietly for a moment, then spoke again, his voice soft and full of understanding. "Because I'm here to help you find your way. You don't have to carry everything on your own. I'm here to walk with you, to remind you of the strength you already have inside of you."

Logan stared at Ari, feeling a strange sense of relief wash over him. It was as if everything he had been holding onto—his doubts, his fears, his uncertainties—were suddenly a little lighter. He didn't fully understand what was happening, but for the first time in a long while, he didn't feel so alone.

"But… why now?" Logan asked.

Ari's gaze never wavered. "Because now is when you need me most. Now is when you're ready to listen."

Logan swallowed hard, the weight of Ari's words settling over him. Maybe he was ready. Maybe that's why the lion had appeared now, of all times— because Logan was finally ready to face whatever was coming next.

For a long moment, they sat in silence, the quiet of the evening settling around them. Logan didn't know what the future held, but with Ari by his side, he felt like maybe—just maybe—he was going to be okay.

"Will you stay?" Logan asked, his voice quiet but hopeful.

Ari smiled. "As long as you need me, I'll be here."

Reflection Questions:

1. Have you ever felt lost or unsure of who you are? How did you handle it?

2. What or who in your life gives you strength, like Ari does for Logan?

3. How can you learn to trust that inner voice that reminds you of your worth, even when you feel weak or uncertain?

4. What makes you feel grounded when life feels chaotic?

Quote:
"Sometimes, the strongest people are the ones who hear the quietest whispers inside themselves." – Unknown

Bible Verse:
"The Lord will fight for you; you need only to be still." – Exodus 14:14

You are brave.

CHAPTER 2

A Friend in the Shadows

The next morning, Logan woke up feeling strangely different. The world outside his window looked the same—the sun casting light across the streets, the trees swaying gently in the breeze—but something inside him had shifted. He remembered Ari, and for a moment, he wondered if the lion had just been a dream.

But when Logan walked downstairs, the familiar golden eyes of the lion were waiting for him at the base of the stairs.

"You're real," Logan whispered, almost to himself.

Ari nodded, his eyes twinkling. "I told you I'd be here."

Logan stood there for a moment, still trying to wrap his mind around everything. A talking lion, here in his house, just for him? It seemed impossible, but at the same time, Logan couldn't help but feel a strange comfort. Maybe he didn't need to understand everything just yet. Maybe it was enough that Ari was here.

Later that day, Logan sat at lunch with his friends.

The school cafeteria was loud, filled with the usual chatter and chaos. Daniel, Lucas, and a few others were deep in conversation about the upcoming weekend, talking about plans, parties, and projects. Logan listened, but his mind was elsewhere. He couldn't stop thinking about Ari.

"You're still coming to Lucas's, right?" Daniel asked, pulling Logan back to the present.

Logan blinked. "Uh, yeah… I guess."

Lucas raised an eyebrow. "You guess? Come on, man. You've been kind of out of it lately."

Logan shifted in his seat, feeling the pressure to say yes, even though he wasn't sure if he really wanted to go. It wasn't that he didn't like his friends—it was just that lately, everything felt… overwhelming. The constant expectations, the pressure to fit in, to be part of the crowd—it was starting to weigh on him.

Ari's voice echoed softly in his mind: "You don't have to carry everything on your own."

Logan glanced around the table, feeling the familiar tug of wanting to please everyone. But this time, something inside him shifted. He didn't have to say yes. He didn't have to go along with what everyone else wanted.

"Actually, I think I might have some stuff going on at home," Logan said, his voice steady but unsure. "I might have to skip this one."

Lucas frowned, clearly disappointed. "Really? You've been missing a lot lately."

Logan's stomach tightened, but he took a deep breath, remembering what Ari had said. "Yeah. I just… need some time."

That afternoon, Logan found himself walking home with Ari beside him.

"You're learning," Ari said, his voice gentle.

"Learning what?" Logan asked, glancing down at the lion.

Ari smiled. "Learning to set boundaries. Learning that it's okay to say no."

Logan sighed. "Yeah, but now I feel like I let them down. Like I'm always the one saying no."

Ari tilted his head. "It's not about letting people down. It's about being true to what you need. Sometimes the world will ask too much of you, and it's okay to say you're not ready. You don't have to be everything for everyone."

Logan looked ahead, feeling the weight on his shoulders lift slightly. "But what if they stop inviting me? What if I end up alone?"

Ari's gaze softened. "You won't be alone. The people who truly care about you will understand. And sometimes, saying no makes room for the things that truly matter."

Logan didn't respond right away, letting Ari's words sink in. He had never thought about it that way before. The pressure to be part of everything, to say yes to every invitation, had always felt like a necessary part of life. But maybe… maybe it didn't have to be.

Later that evening, Logan sat in his room, staring out the window.

The sun was setting, casting a warm golden light over everything. For the first time in a while, Logan felt like he could breathe. He wasn't worried about what his friends thought, or about keeping up with everyone else. He had made a decision that felt right for him, and that was enough.
Ari lay quietly by his bed, watching him with those knowing eyes.

"You're not as lost as you think, Logan," Ari said softly. "You just need to trust yourself a little more."

Logan smiled, feeling a sense of peace wash over him. "Yeah. I think I'm starting to get that."

Reflection Questions:

1. Have you ever had someone in your life that supports you quietly, like Ari supports Logan? How does their presence make a difference for you?

2. How can you be more aware of the people around you who need support, even when they don't ask for it?

3. What does friendship mean to you? How can you be a friend who is present, even in the quiet moments?

Quote:
"True friendship comes when the silence between two people is comfortable."
– David Tyson

Bible Verse:
"A friend loves at all times, and a brother is born for a time of adversity."
– Proverbs 17:17

You are strong.

CHAPTER 3

The Fear of Failing

The school day had come to an end, and Logan slumped into his usual spot at the back of the bus. He pressed his forehead against the cool window and watched the streets blur by as the bus bounced along the road. Ari hopped up onto the seat next to him, settling in comfortably with a soft thud.

Logan's mind was racing, his thoughts tangled in a mess of frustration and worry. No matter how hard he tried, it felt like nothing was good enough—not for his parents, not for his teachers, and especially not for himself.

"You've been awfully quiet since class ended," Ari said, his eyes observing Logan closely. "What's on your mind?"

Logan sighed, his breath fogging up the window. "It's just… everything feels like too much, you know? It's like I'm being set up to fail."

Ari tilted his head, listening. "Fail at what?"

"Everything," Logan muttered. "I got a C on my math test, which is just going to disappoint my parents. And then, there's this project for history, and I don't even know where to start. My coach keeps pushing me harder at practice, and I can't keep up. It's like everyone expects me to be this… perfect version of myself. But I'm not."

Ari sat in silence for a moment, letting Logan's words sink in. The bus rumbled on, and the soft hum of conversations around them seemed distant.

"It's okay to fail sometimes, you know," Ari said, his voice calm but sure. "Failure isn't the end of the world. It's part of figuring things out."

Logan turned to look at him, frowning. "Yeah, well, it sure feels like the end of the world when everyone's disappointed in you."

Ari's tail swished thoughtfully. "Maybe it's not about them. Maybe it's about how you see yourself. You're putting all this pressure on yourself because you think you need to be perfect. But what if you're allowed to make mistakes?"

Logan looked back out the window, biting his lip. "But what if I fail too much? What if I can't catch up?"

Ari hopped down from the seat and stood in front of Logan, his eyes steady. "You won't. Because failure isn't the end—it's just part of the process. You'll learn from it, and then you'll do better next time. You can't avoid mistakes, Logan. No one can."

Logan's hand tightened around the strap of his backpack. "But what if… what if I let everyone down?"

Ari softened his gaze. "You're not living your life for them. You're living it for you."

Logan sat with those words for a moment. He'd been so wrapped up in worrying about what other people thought of him—his parents, his teachers, his friends—that he hadn't even stopped to consider what he wanted for himself.

The truth was, he didn't even know.

"Maybe you're right," Logan said quietly. "But it's hard to think like that when it feels like everyone's waiting for me to mess up."

Ari nodded. "I know it's hard. But you've got to give yourself some room to breathe. No one expects you to be perfect. And if they do, that's their problem, not yours."

Logan gave a small nod, feeling the tightness in his chest ease just a little. "I guess… I just don't want to fail."

"Then try your best," Ari said, "but understand that failing doesn't mean you're a failure. You're still growing, still learning. You've got time."

The bus pulled up to Logan's stop, and he stood up, slinging his backpack over his shoulder. He felt a little lighter, like maybe he didn't have to carry the world's expectations on his back anymore.

As they stepped off the bus and walked toward Logan's house, Ari stayed by his side, silent but present.

Logan kicked at the pebbles on the sidewalk, glancing down at Ari. "You're really good at this, you know."

Ari grinned, his tail swishing behind him. "Good at what?"

"Helping me not freak out," Logan said with a small laugh. "I mean, I'm still freaked out, but… less."

Ari smiled. "That's all part of the process, too. You don't have to get it all figured out at once."

Logan felt the weight of his backpack and the day lift, even just a little. The pressure might not go away overnight, but knowing that it was okay to fail—that it was okay to be unsure—made it feel a bit more manageable.

As they reached Logan's house, Ari paused at the front step and looked up at him. "You're going to be okay, you know that, right?"

Logan smiled, a real smile this time. "Yeah. I think I'm starting to believe that."

And as Logan opened the door, Ari followed him inside, knowing that, step by step, Logan would find his way—even if it meant taking a few wrong turns along the way.

Reflection Questions:

1. What challenges in your life make you feel small or powerless? How can you draw on inner strength to face them?

2. How do you define strength? Is it something loud and visible, or can it be quiet and steady like Ari's presence?

3. What helps you stay strong when you face difficulties, even when you don't feel ready for them?

Quote:
"Courage doesn't always roar. Sometimes courage is the quiet voice at the end of the day saying, 'I will try again tomorrow.'" – Mary Anne Radmacher

Bible Verse:
"Be strong and courageous. Do not be afraid; do not be discouraged, for the Lord your God will be with you wherever you go." – Joshua 1:9

You are capable.

CHAPTER 4

When the World Feels Too Big

It was Friday afternoon, and the halls of Riverside High were buzzing with the usual end-of-week excitement. Students rushed out of their last classes, ready to head to the mall, hang out with friends, or just crash at home. Logan, however, walked a little slower, his mind preoccupied.

Ari trotted beside him, his quiet presence always a comfort. "What's up, Logan? You've been quiet all day."

Logan shrugged, adjusting his backpack. "Just thinking about going home."

Ari glanced up at him. He knew Logan's home life wasn't always easy. His parents were supportive but had high expectations, especially since his older brother, Nick, had set such a high bar. Logan often felt like he was living in Nick's shadow, always trying to prove himself but never feeling like he measured up.

As they walked out of the school gates, Logan's friend Ethan jogged up behind them, calling out, "Yo, Logan! You coming to the game tonight?"

Logan hesitated. He had been planning to go, but now he wasn't so sure. His math grade was still bothering him, and he knew his parents would ask about it the moment he walked through the door. Plus, his little sister, Emma, had been struggling with her own schoolwork, and Logan felt like he should stay home and help her instead.

"I don't know, man. I might skip it," Logan said, trying to sound casual.

Ethan frowned. "What? You're always at the games. What's going on?"

Logan shifted uncomfortably. He didn't feel like getting into everything right now—not in front of the school. "Just a lot going on at home," he muttered.

Ari stayed quiet, watching the interaction. He could tell that Logan was holding back, not wanting to admit how much pressure he felt from his parents or how exhausted he was trying to juggle everything. Ethan looked like he wanted to say more but just nodded.

"Alright, hit me up if you change your mind," Ethan said before turning to join a group of their friends.

Logan exhaled slowly. "Sometimes I wish things were simpler, you know?"

Ari nodded as they started walking again. "You don't always have to carry everything on your own, Logan. You've got friends—and family."

Logan gave a half-hearted shrug. "Yeah, but my family expects a lot. I don't want to disappoint them."

By the time they reached Logan's house, the weight of the week felt heavy on his shoulders. Ari padded quietly beside him as Logan opened the front door. His mom was in the kitchen, chopping vegetables for dinner, and his dad was sitting at the table, looking over some papers.

"Hey, Logan," his mom called over her shoulder. "How was school?"

"Fine," Logan replied, trying to sound as neutral as possible. He dropped his backpack by the stairs and glanced over at his dad, who was already eyeing him with that familiar look of expectation.

"How'd the math test go?" his dad asked without looking up from the papers.

Logan's stomach tightened. He knew this question was coming, but it didn't make it any easier. "It was okay," he said quietly.

"Okay?" His dad finally looked up. "You said you were ready for that test. Did you get your grade yet?"

Logan nodded, avoiding eye contact. "Yeah. I got a C."

A heavy silence filled the room. His dad's expression tightened, and his mom paused in her chopping. Logan could feel the disappointment before anyone even said anything.

"A C?" His dad's voice was calm but laced with disappointment. "What happened? I thought we went over the material together."

"I know," Logan said quickly, his heart pounding. "I just… I don't know. I messed up on a couple of questions."

His dad sighed and leaned back in his chair. "You've got to do better, Logan. I know you're capable of more than that."

Logan bit his lip, feeling the familiar sting of failure. He knew his parents only wanted the best for him, but the constant pressure was suffocating. Ari, sensing the tension, stepped closer, nudging Logan's leg with his nose.

"Maybe next time, we can study together," Logan's mom said gently, trying to ease the tension. "It's not the end of the world, honey."

But to Logan, it felt like it was.

He nodded, not trusting himself to speak. "I'm gonna go upstairs and help Emma with her homework," he muttered, grabbing his backpack and heading up the stairs before anyone could say anything else.

Ari followed silently, his presence a quiet reminder that Logan wasn't alone.

Upstairs, Logan knocked on his little sister's door before stepping inside. Emma was sitting at her desk, staring blankly at her math workbook, clearly frustrated.

"Need some help?" Logan asked, trying to sound upbeat.

Emma glanced over at him, her face brightening just a little. "Yeah. I'm stuck on this problem, and I don't get it."

Logan pulled up a chair beside her, glancing at the problem. "Alright, let's figure it out together."

As they worked through the math problem, Logan couldn't help but notice the way Emma's shoulders relaxed when she realized she was getting it right.

Her frustration melted away, and by the time they finished, she was smiling again.

"Thanks, Logan," Emma said, her eyes shining with relief. "I was starting to think I was never going to get it."

Logan smiled softly. "Hey, we all get stuck sometimes. It doesn't mean you're not smart."

Emma nodded, and Ari padded up to her, resting his head on her lap. Emma giggled and patted Ari's head. "You always know how to make me feel better," she said, looking at Ari like he understood every word.

Ari looked up at her with his warm, golden eyes and gave a small nod, almost as if to say, That's what I'm here for.

Logan watched the interaction, feeling a sense of calm wash over him. Helping Emma had been a small thing, but it reminded him that sometimes, even when you felt like you were failing, you could still make a difference.

Maybe that's what Ari had been trying to tell him all along.

Reflection Questions:

1. Have you ever felt like Logan—overwhelmed by everything around you? What helped you get through that feeling?

2. How can you focus on one step at a time when everything feels too overwhelming?

3. What reminders can you give yourself when life feels out of control?

Quote:
"When everything feels like an uphill struggle, just think of the view from the top." – Unknown

Bible Verse:
"Come to me, all you who are weary and burdened, and I will give you rest."
– Matthew 11:28

Stay determined.

Be fearless today.

44

CHAPTER 5

The Fear of Missing Out
(FOMO)

Logan sat cross-legged on his bed, his phone glowing in the dim light of his room. The school day was over, and after helping Emma with her homework, he finally had some time to himself. But instead of feeling relaxed, he found himself scrolling through his social media feed, feeling that familiar knot of anxiety tightening in his chest.

Ari lay at the foot of the bed, his eyes half-closed but still aware of Logan's mood. The light from the phone reflected in Logan's eyes as he scrolled through posts—his friends hanging out at the mall, the basketball team celebrating after practice, and endless streams of perfect photos, smiles, and lives that seemed a lot more put together than his own.

"You know staring at that screen isn't going to make you feel any better," Ari said softly, not even bothering to open his eyes.

Logan sighed, not looking away from his phone. "I know. It's just… everyone seems like they're living their best lives, and here I am, barely getting through the week."

Ari shifted and sat up, padding over to Logan's side. "That's because they only show the best parts. You don't see what's really going on behind the screen."

Logan frowned. He knew Ari was right, but it didn't make the feeling any less real. "Yeah, but it still feels like I'm falling behind. Like I'm the only one who doesn't have it all together."

He stared at a picture of Ethan and some of their other friends from school, all smiling in a photo they'd posted just a few minutes ago. They were at the basketball game—the game Logan had decided to skip.

Maybe I should've gone, he thought to himself. Now I just look like I'm not part of the group.

Ari nudged him gently. "You don't have to be everywhere to matter, Logan."

Logan set his phone down, rubbing his temples. "I know, but… it's hard not to feel like I'm missing out. Like I'm not enough."

Ari climbed onto the bed beside him, his soft fur brushing against Logan's arm. "It's called FOMO, right? Fear of missing out. But you're not really missing out. What you're seeing isn't the whole story."

Logan nodded, but the feeling of inadequacy still gnawed at him. It wasn't just tonight's game. It was everything—his friends, the way they all seemed to have the perfect social lives, and even the accounts of random people he didn't even know. Everyone was living these exciting, Instagram-worthy lives, and he felt like he was just… there. In the background.

Meanwhile, downstairs, Emma was facing her own social media battle.

She sat on the living room couch, her phone clutched in her hands. Her friends had been talking all day about this new challenge that had gone viral—one where you had to post a selfie and get as many likes as possible within an hour. Whoever got the most likes would "win," whatever that meant.

Emma wasn't sure she wanted to play, but all her friends were doing it, and she didn't want to be the only one left out. She stared at the camera on her phone, feeling a knot in her stomach. She didn't like taking selfies. She always felt awkward, like no matter what angle she used or how many filters she applied, she just didn't look as good as everyone else.

Ari padded into the living room, his ears perking up as he noticed Emma staring at her phone, the same troubled look Logan had upstairs.

"You okay, Emma?" Ari asked, sitting down next to her.

Emma sighed. "I don't know. There's this challenge going around, and I feel like I have to do it. But I don't really want to."

Ari tilted his head. "Then why do it?"

"Because all my friends are," Emma said, her voice frustrated. "I don't want to be the only one not playing along. I'll look stupid."

Ari looked up at her, his golden eyes soft. "You know you don't have to do something just because everyone else is doing it, right?"

Emma frowned. "Yeah, but if I don't, I'll get left out. Everyone's going to post their selfies, and they'll probably get tons of likes. I'll be the only one without a post. It's like… if you don't play along, people forget about you."

Ari rested his head on her lap, offering silent support. "People who care about you won't forget about you just because you didn't post a picture. You're more than how many likes you get, Emma."

Emma stared at her phone, her finger hovering over the camera button. "I just wish it didn't feel like such a big deal."

"It only feels that way because that's how social media works," Ari said gently. "It makes you think that likes and comments are what matter, but they're not. You matter, just as you are."

Emma put her phone down and looked at Ari. "It's hard not to care, though."

"I know," Ari said. "But think about this—do you really want to be part of something that makes you feel bad about yourself? You don't have to prove anything to anyone. You're enough, just being you."

Emma sat quietly, her mind racing. She knew Ari was right. Deep down, she knew she didn't want to play this game. It wasn't who she was. But standing up to the pressure? That was hard.

She looked down at Ari and gave a small smile. "Thanks, Ari. I think I needed to hear that."

Ari wagged his tail gently. "That's what I'm here for."

Later that night, upstairs in Logan's room, Ari watched as Logan picked up his phone again.

"I'm not going to the game," Logan said, almost to himself. "But I feel like I should've. Like I'm missing something."

Ari jumped onto the bed and curled up beside him. "You're not missing anything that really matters, Logan. The people who care about you? They're not going to care if you're at every game, every hangout. They'll care that you're real with them."

Logan sighed, finally putting his phone down. "Social media sucks sometimes."

Ari chuckled softly. "It can be tricky, yeah. But remember, what you see on there isn't the whole story. People only show the parts they want others to see. Don't let it make you feel like you're less than who you are."

Logan nodded, feeling the weight of the day slowly lifting. "Yeah. I guess I just need to stop comparing myself."

"Exactly," Ari said with a grin. "You're doing just fine. You're enough, Logan. And so is Emma."

Reflection Questions:

1. Have you ever found yourself comparing your life to what you see on social media?

- How does it affect your self-esteem when you do?

2. Do you feel obligated to join in on trends or challenges online just to fit in?

- How can you remind yourself that you don't need to do everything others are doing?

3. What can you do to protect your mental health when social media makes you feel left out or not good enough?

Quote:
"Comparison is the thief of joy." – Theodore Roosevelt

Bible Verse:
"Do not conform to the pattern of this world, but be transformed by the renewing of your mind." – Romans 12:2

Trust your confidence.

You are brilliant.

CHAPTER 6

The Power of Quiet Courage

53

It was Saturday afternoon, and the sun was shining brightly over the neighborhood. Logan sat on the front steps of his house, watching as a few kids rode their bikes down the street. His phone buzzed beside him, but he ignored it. After the pressure of the past week, he needed a break from social media—and from feeling like he had to keep up with everyone.

Ari lay stretched out on the grass nearby, soaking up the sun. He kept a watchful eye on Logan, sensing that even though they weren't talking, there was still something heavy on his friend's mind.

"You thinking about the game last night?" Ari asked casually, lifting his head to look at Logan.

Logan shrugged. "Kind of. I keep seeing the pictures everyone posted on social media. I didn't miss anything major, but… it still feels like I did."

Ari tilted his head. "Sometimes it feels like the world moves on without us when we step back, huh?"

Logan nodded, picking at a loose thread on his jeans. "Yeah, exactly. It's like… if you're not part of it, then you're just invisible. And sometimes, that's what I feel like—just invisible."

Ari moved closer, his golden eyes warm and full of understanding. "But being invisible isn't always bad, Logan. Sometimes it gives you space to figure out who you really are, without all the noise."

Logan considered that for a moment, looking out at the quiet street. Maybe Ari was right. Being away from the constant stream of social media and everyone's expectations had given him time to think. But it didn't make it easier to deal with the nagging feeling that he was being left behind.

Just then, Emma stepped out onto the porch, her phone in hand. "Hey, Logan? Can I talk to you for a sec?"

Logan looked up at his little sister, noticing the worry in her eyes. "Sure, what's up?"

Emma glanced at Ari before sitting down beside her brother. She hesitated for a moment, then showed Logan her phone. "It's about that selfie challenge I told you about."

Logan frowned. "Did you end up doing it?"

Emma shook her head, but her hands fidgeted with the phone. "No, I didn't. But now I feel like everyone's ignoring me because of it. It's like they've all moved on, and I'm not part of the group anymore."

Logan took a deep breath, feeling a pang of protectiveness for his sister. He knew how tough that feeling could be, especially at her age. "Em, listen. Social media makes everything feel like it's more important than it is. But your real friends? They don't care if you do some dumb challenge or not. If they're ignoring you over something like that, maybe they're not really worth worrying about."

Emma blinked, surprised by Logan's advice. She'd expected him to brush it off, but there was something in his tone that made her feel like he really understood.

Ari padded over to Emma, resting his head on her lap. "You know, Emma, sometimes people get so caught up in what they think matters—like likes or challenges—that they forget the things that really matter. You don't have to play their game to be valued."

Emma ran her hand through Ari's soft fur, her heart feeling a little lighter. "I guess I just wanted to fit in."

Logan put his arm around her shoulders. "I get it. I really do. But fitting in doesn't mean you have to change who you are. It just means finding the people who accept you for you."

Ari lifted his head and smiled. "Exactly. And the ones who stick around? They're the ones worth keeping."

Later that evening, Logan found himself at his friend Ethan's house.

Ethan had invited a few people over to hang out and play video games. Logan had been hesitant to come at first, especially after feeling disconnected from everyone, but Ari had nudged him into it.

"Sometimes you just need to show up," Ari had said. "You might be surprised by what happens."

Now sitting in Ethan's living room, Logan was glad he'd listened to Ari. The familiar banter of his friends, the sound of laughter, and the glow of the video game screen all felt comforting. But as the night went on, Logan noticed something he hadn't before.

Ethan, usually the life of the party, seemed… off. His jokes weren't landing the same way, and there was a quietness to him that Logan couldn't quite place. After everyone else had left or moved into the kitchen, Logan sat beside Ethan on the couch, with Ari lying quietly at their feet.

"You good, man?" Logan asked, his voice low enough so the others wouldn't overhear.

Ethan hesitated, his eyes glued to the game screen. "Yeah… I'm fine."
Logan raised an eyebrow. "Come on. I know when something's up."

Ethan sighed, dropping the controller into his lap. "It's just… social media, you know? It's like, everyone expects me to always be 'on,' you know? Like I have to be this perfect version of myself all the time, or people lose interest. And lately, I feel like no matter what I post, it's not good enough."

Logan felt a wave of understanding wash over him. He'd been there—heck, he was still there some days. The constant pressure to be "perfect" on social media, to never let anyone see the cracks. It was exhausting.

"You don't have to be perfect, Ethan," Logan said, leaning back against the couch. "I mean, we're your friends. We don't care about your posts or how many likes you get. We just care about you."

Ethan ran a hand through his hair. "I know that, but… it's hard not to feel like you're falling behind when everyone else seems to be killing it."

Ari looked up at Ethan, his gentle presence like a grounding force in the room. "Everyone's fighting their own battles, Ethan. What you see online is just a fraction of the story. No one's got it all together."

Ethan gave a small laugh, but it sounded tired. "Yeah, I guess you're right. It's just… hard."

Logan nodded. "It is. But you've got people who've got your back, okay? You don't have to put on a mask for us."

Ethan looked over at Logan, his expression softening. "Thanks, man. I didn't realize how much I needed to hear that."

Ari wagged his tail gently, sensing the tension lift. "That's what friends are for. Sometimes we all need to drop the mask."

As the night wore on, Logan, Ethan, and their friends played games, laughed, and talked about everything from school to their plans for the weekend. But there was a new understanding between them—one that didn't rely on social media, filters, or the need to impress. It was real.

And as Logan headed home that night, with Ari by his side, he realized something important: even when the world outside felt overwhelming, he had people—real people—who cared. And that was enough.

Reflection Questions:

1. What does quiet courage mean to you? How can you show strength, even when you feel afraid?

2. How do you face your fears, even when they seem overwhelming?

3. What small acts of bravery have you noticed in your own life? How can you celebrate those moments?

Quote:
"Courage is not the absence of fear, but the triumph over it." – Nelson Mandela

Bible Verse:
"Even though I walk through the darkest valley, I will fear no evil, for you are with me; your rod and your staff, they comfort me." – Psalm 23:4

Believe in yourself.

You've got this!

CHAPTER 7

The Pressure to Belong

It was Monday afternoon, and Logan stood outside the school gym, waiting for Ethan and their friends. The school day had been long, and all Logan wanted was to go home and crash. But today, there was something else tugging at him—something he couldn't quite shake off.

As students filed out of the building, Logan caught sight of Ethan and their usual crew. They were laughing about something, but as Logan got closer, he noticed a different energy between them.

"Yo, Logan!" Ethan called out, waving him over. "We're heading to the park after school to hang. You down?"

Logan hesitated. "The park? Isn't that where all the older guys hang out?"

Ethan shrugged, his expression casual. "Yeah, they're usually there. But it's no big deal. We've been hanging with them lately. It's cool."

Logan shifted uncomfortably. The park was known as a place where the older high schoolers—seniors mostly—would go to smoke, drink, and sometimes cause trouble. It wasn't really his scene, and he wasn't sure he wanted to get involved.

Ari, who had been quietly watching from the sidelines, stepped closer. "Logan, you don't have to go if it doesn't feel right."

But before Logan could respond, one of the other guys chimed in. "Come on, Logan. You've been dodging us all weekend. What, you don't want to hang out anymore?"

Logan felt his stomach twist. He hadn't meant to skip out on so many things lately. Between school, his parents, and trying to keep his grades up, he hadn't had the energy to deal with the pressure of always being "on." But now, standing in front of his friends, he felt that familiar pull—the need to fit in, to be part of the group.

"I don't know, man," Logan said, scratching the back of his head. "I've got a lot of homework and stuff."

Ethan gave him a playful shove. "It's just a couple of hours. You can do your homework later. Besides, you don't want to be the only one missing out, do you?"

Logan hesitated. He knew Ethan didn't mean any harm, but the pressure was real. If he didn't go, it would feel like he was being left out—again. And with everything he'd missed over the weekend, he couldn't afford to lose his spot in the group.

Ari nudged his leg, his voice calm but firm. "You don't have to go just because they expect you to, Logan. Trust your gut."

Logan looked at Ari, then back at his friends. He knew Ari was right, but saying no felt impossible. He didn't want to seem uncool or like he was too scared to hang out. The older guys at the park weren't exactly known for being welcoming, but everyone was doing it. And if everyone was doing it, then maybe it wasn't as bad as it seemed.

"Alright," Logan said finally. "I'll go."

At the park, Logan quickly realized his mistake.

The moment they arrived, the older guys were already there, leaning against their cars, passing around cigarettes and cans of beer. Logan's heart raced as he followed Ethan and the others to where the group was gathered.

"Hey, look who decided to join us!" one of the older guys said, smirking as Logan approached. "You're with Ethan's crew, right?"

Logan nodded, trying to seem relaxed even though his nerves were screaming at him to leave.

The older guys didn't waste any time. Within minutes, someone offered Logan a beer. His hands felt clammy as he took it, his mind racing. He didn't drink—he didn't even want to—but standing there with everyone watching, he felt trapped.

Ari appeared beside him, his presence a steady reminder that he didn't have to do this. "You can walk away, Logan," Ari said quietly. "You don't have to prove anything to them."

Logan swallowed hard, his hand gripping the can tightly. His friends were already cracking open their drinks, laughing and blending in with the older crowd. They looked so at ease, like they belonged. But Logan felt like an outsider, a kid trying to be something he wasn't.

"Come on, man," one of the older guys called out. "What are you waiting for?"

Logan glanced down at Ari, who was watching him closely, waiting for him to make his choice.

Taking a deep breath, Logan set the can down on the ground. "I'm good," he said, his voice steady despite the tension in his chest.

The older guys raised their eyebrows, but no one said anything. Ethan gave him a curious look but didn't push it. Logan could feel the weight of the decision settling on him, but as Ari stood beside him, he knew he'd made the right call.

Later that evening, Logan and Ethan sat on the swings at the park, the rest of the group still hanging out in the distance.

Ethan glanced at Logan, a small smile playing on his lips. "You know, you didn't have to come today if you didn't want to."

Logan let out a quiet laugh. "Yeah, well… I felt like I had to."

Ethan nodded, kicking at the dirt beneath his feet. "I get it. But you don't, man. You don't have to do what everyone else is doing. I mean, I didn't want to drink either, but… you know how it is."

Logan looked over at his friend, surprised. "You didn't want to?"

Ethan shook his head. "Nah. But everyone else was, and it felt easier to just go along with it."

Logan felt a weight lift off his chest. "Why didn't you just say something?"

Ethan shrugged. "Same reason you didn't. I didn't want to be the odd one out."

Ari padded over to them, his golden eyes filled with understanding. "Sometimes it takes one person saying no to make the rest realize they didn't want to say yes in the first place."

Logan smiled, feeling a sense of relief wash over him. "Yeah. I guess it's just hard to stand out when everyone's pushing you to fit in."

Ethan gave him a grateful look. "Thanks for not going along with it, man. It made it easier for me to say no, too."

Logan nodded, feeling a new sense of confidence in his choice. "We don't have to do what everyone else does, Ethan. We can just… be ourselves."

Ari sat down beside them, his presence a quiet reminder that courage wasn't about going along with the crowd—it was about standing firm, even when it felt like you were standing alone.

Reflection Questions:

1. Have you ever felt pressure to fit in with others, even when it didn't feel right to you? How did you handle it?

2. What can you do to stay true to yourself, even when others expect you to be something you're not?

3. Why do you think it's so hard to go against the crowd sometimes?

Quote:
"It takes courage to grow up and become who you really are." – E.E. Cummings

Bible Verse:
"Do not conform to the pattern of this world, but be transformed by the renewing of your mind." – Romans 12:2

Keep shining bright.

Embrace your courage.

CHAPTER 8

The Invitation

Logan sat at his usual spot in the cafeteria, finishing his lunch when his friend Ethan slid into the seat across from him with a grin.

"Hey, Logan! You know how we were talking about joining a fraternity? Well, guess what—I got us an invite to Tau Delta's rush week!" Ethan's eyes sparkled with excitement.

Logan's heart sank a little. Tau Delta was known for its intense activities and the endless obligations that came with membership. He wasn't sure he wanted to commit to something that big, but he didn't want to let Ethan down. Ethan had been talking about the fraternity all semester, and Logan knew how much it meant to him.

"Oh, wow. That's… awesome," Logan said, trying to sound enthusiastic.

Ethan gave him a playful punch on the shoulder. "You don't look excited! C'mon, man, this is going to be amazing. Imagine all the connections we'll make and the parties! Plus, I need you there with me."

Logan forced a smile, nodding along. "Yeah… sure."

As the week went on, Logan found himself buried under invitations, late-night texts, and fraternity tasks that seemed to come out of nowhere. Every time he tried to focus on his studies or relax, his phone would buzz with a message from Ethan or someone from Tau Delta. They expected him to be at every event, to help with every errand. The pressure was building up, and it felt suffocating.

By Friday, he was exhausted. He wanted a quiet night, but Ethan texted him about another fraternity meetup. Logan hesitated, staring at his phone, his heart pounding. He knew he needed a break, but he didn't want Ethan or the others to think he wasn't committed or, worse, that he wasn't a good friend.

Just as Logan slumped back on his bed, feeling overwhelmed, he felt a familiar warmth by his side. It was Ari, his lion guide, with his wise, gentle eyes and a calm presence that instantly soothed Logan's racing thoughts. "Rough week, isn't it?" Ari asked softly.

Logan sighed. "I feel like I'm letting everyone down, Ari. I just wanted to make Ethan happy, but now it's like I have no life of my own. I can't keep up with this and still be… me."

Ari tilted his head, considering Logan's words carefully. "Tell me, Logan, why do you feel like you have to be there for everyone, every time?"

Logan thought about it. "I guess… I just don't want to disappoint Ethan. I don't want him to think I'm not a good friend if I don't join."

Ari sat down beside him, his deep golden eyes fixed on Logan's. "Being a good friend doesn't mean sacrificing your own peace or constantly pushing yourself to meet others' expectations. True friendship is about respect— respecting each other's needs and boundaries."

Logan glanced at his phone, where Ethan's latest text waited. "But what if he thinks I don't care about him? What if this ruins our friendship?"

Ari placed a gentle paw on Logan's hand. "Real friends understand when you need time for yourself. They value you for who you are, not for what you can do for them. If you keep giving all of yourself away, what will be left for you?" Logan took a deep breath, nodding slowly. Ari was right. He was exhausted, not because he didn't care about Ethan, but because he had given so much that he was forgetting to take care of himself.

Feeling a renewed sense of clarity, Logan picked up his phone and texted Ethan.

"Hey, man. I'm all for supporting you with the fraternity, but I've got to be honest—I need some downtime this weekend. I've been feeling a bit overwhelmed. Hope you understand."

Within seconds, Ethan replied: "Of course, bro! I didn't realize it was too much for you. Take the weekend off, no worries!"

Logan felt a wave of relief wash over him. He hadn't expected Ethan to understand so easily, but he realized now that setting boundaries didn't make him a bad friend—it made him a healthier one.

Reflection Questions:

1. Have you ever felt pressured to meet someone else's expectations? How did it affect you?

2. What are some ways you can communicate your own boundaries with friends?

3. How can respecting your own needs make you a better friend?

Quote:
"True friendship is not about being inseparable; it's about being able to let each other grow while still being close."

Bible Verse:
"Let each of you look not only to his own interests but also to the interests of others." – Philippians 2:4

You are unstoppable.

CHAPTER 9

Finding Your Passion Amid Distractions

It was career day at school, and the hallways buzzed with excitement. Logan's classmates were chattering about their dreams and future goals. Some talked about becoming doctors or engineers, others about starting businesses or traveling the world. Logan felt a twinge of anxiety—he had no idea what he wanted to do. It seemed like everyone else had a clear path, while he was… lost.

At lunch, his friends started talking about their own plans. Ethan wanted to go into finance like his dad, and Sarah was planning to study art. When they turned to Logan, he shrugged, trying to play it cool. "Not sure yet. I've got time, right?"

But inside, Logan felt the pressure mounting. Everyone had their "thing." Why didn't he?

Over the next few weeks, Logan tried to figure it out by joining various clubs and activities his friends recommended. He went to the basketball team tryouts with Ethan, but sports just weren't his thing. He tried photography club with Sarah, but felt out of place there too. He even considered joining the school's debate team after hearing his friends talk about how good it looked on college applications, but his heart just wasn't in it.

It seemed like every path he explored was someone else's idea, and every time he tried something new, it felt like he was just going through the motions.

One evening, feeling more confused than ever, Logan sat outside on his porch, staring up at the stars. Just then, he felt a presence beside him. He didn't need to look—it was Ari, his trusted lion guide.

"Can't sleep?" Ari asked in his usual calm tone.

Logan shook his head. "I just… I don't know what I'm supposed to do with my life, Ari. Everyone else seems to know what they want. I keep trying different things, but nothing feels… right."

Ari settled down next to him, looking thoughtful. "Tell me, Logan, when was the last time you did something just because it made you happy, without worrying about what anyone else thought?"

Logan frowned, thinking back. He remembered when he was younger, spending hours building things with his Legos. He'd lose track of time, completely absorbed in creating. But now, he felt he had to pursue something "impressive," something that would make others proud.

"I don't know," Logan admitted. "It's hard to know what I actually enjoy when I'm always trying to meet other people's expectations."

Ari nodded. "Sometimes, the noise around us drowns out our own inner voice. Discovering what you love takes quiet and patience. It's not about choosing something that impresses others; it's about finding what makes you feel alive."

Ari suggested that Logan take some time each week to explore things on his own terms—without worrying about how it would look to others or if it would lead anywhere big. The next day, Logan took his advice to heart. He began trying different activities just to see how they felt. He spent a Saturday morning hiking alone, letting his mind wander. He tried cooking a new recipe, discovering he liked experimenting in the kitchen. Slowly, he realized that he loved creative projects, especially those he could do at his own pace. He wasn't following a script, and for the first time, it felt freeing. Logan didn't feel pressured to "fit in" or to find his passion instantly. Instead, he started enjoying the process of learning more about himself.

By the end of the month, Logan still didn't have all the answers, but he had something even better: the courage to keep exploring without rushing. Ari's advice helped him see that passion doesn't always arrive in a flash; sometimes, it's uncovered slowly, through small steps and quiet moments.

Reflection Questions:

1. Have you ever felt pressured to follow a certain path because of what others expected?

2. What activities make you feel happy, even if they aren't "impressive" to others?

3. How can you take small steps to discover what you truly enjoy, without rushing?

Quote:
"Passion is not something you find by following the crowd; it's discovered in moments of quiet and curiosity."

Bible Verse:
"Commit to the Lord whatever you do, and he will establish your plans."
– Proverbs 16:3

You're doing amazing.

Greatness is within you.

CHAPTER 10

Dealing with Disappointment

Logan had been training hard for the school's basketball team tryouts. He wasn't the tallest player, nor the fastest, but he poured his heart into every practice, spending hours after school shooting hoops and improving his game. He had dreamed of playing for the team ever since he started high school, imagining the thrill of running down the court with the crowd cheering.

When tryouts finally came, Logan gave it everything he had. He could almost taste the victory and felt certain that his hard work would pay off. But when the team list was posted, Logan's name wasn't on it.

He stared at the paper, his stomach dropping. All his hours of practice, his sacrifices, his hopes—they felt meaningless. He walked home, his mind swirling with disappointment and frustration.

At home, Logan locked himself in his room, replaying the tryouts in his mind, wondering what he did wrong. His friends on the team texted him, trying to be supportive, but it only made him feel worse. It seemed like everyone knew he'd failed, and he couldn't shake the feeling that he'd let himself—and everyone else—down.

As he lay on his bed, staring up at the ceiling, he heard a soft, familiar sound by the window. Turning, he saw Ari's golden eyes watching him from the sill. Logan didn't even feel like talking, but somehow, Ari always knew when to show up.

Ari climbed onto Logan's bed, sitting quietly beside him, sensing Logan's sadness without needing any words.

After a long silence, Ari finally spoke. "I can see this is weighing on you, Logan. Want to talk about it?"

Logan sat up, sighing. "I worked so hard, Ari. I put in all that effort, and for what? It feels like… all of it was just a waste. Maybe I'm not cut out for this after all."

Ari's gaze softened, his eyes full of understanding. "It's natural to feel disappointed when things don't go as planned. But tell me, did you really learn nothing from this experience?"

Logan frowned, thinking. "Well… I guess I did get a lot better. I'm stronger than I was before I started training. But still, it's not enough. I didn't make the team."

Ari nodded thoughtfully. "Sometimes, success isn't the only measure of growth. Every step you took, every hour you spent, made you better—not just as a player, but as a person. This journey wasn't a waste just because it didn't end the way you imagined."

Ari continued, "Many people face setbacks, Logan. It's part of life. The difference is in how you choose to respond. You can let this disappointment define you, or you can see it as one part of a much bigger story. Growth often happens in the moments that feel hardest."

Logan considered Ari's words, realizing that while he hadn't achieved his goal, he had become more resilient, more disciplined, and even more skilled in the process. It wasn't what he had planned, but maybe Ari was right—there was value in the journey, even without the reward.

After their talk, Logan decided to keep practicing. Not to prove anything to others, but because he loved the game. Over time, he began helping younger players who wanted to improve, sharing his skills and supporting them. He found a new sense of purpose, and in time, his confidence returned. Though he hadn't made the team, his journey took a new, unexpected direction.

Reflection Questions:

1. Can you think of a time when things didn't go as planned? How did it make you feel?

2. How can you find value in the journey, even if it doesn't end the way you hoped?

3. What lessons have you learned from past disappointments that have made you stronger?

Quote:
"Disappointments are often the springboards to greater things, teaching us resilience and helping us grow."

Bible Verse:
"For I know the plans I have for you," declares the Lord, "plans to prosper you and not to harm you, plans to give you hope and a future." – Jeremiah 29:11

Keep going—you're close.

You are remarkable.

CHAPTER 11

Facing Conflict with Kindness

Logan was working on a group project in his history class. His group included his friend Sarah and another classmate, James, who was known for having strong opinions. They'd been assigned to research and present on a controversial historical event, and each group member was responsible for a different part of the presentation.

When they met to go over their progress, Logan noticed that James's section was filled with personal opinions rather than researched facts. Logan, wanting the project to be accurate and well-rounded, suggested they make some changes. But James took it personally.

"What, you think you know better than I do?" James snapped, his face turning red. "Just because you like doing everything by the book doesn't mean I have to."

Logan was taken aback. He hadn't meant to offend James, but he could feel his own frustration rising. Part of him wanted to fire back with a sarcastic response, but he hesitated. He knew it would only make things worse.

Later that day, Logan was sitting alone in the library, still stewing over the argument with James. Suddenly, Ari appeared beside him, his calm presence immediately soothing Logan's nerves.

"Looks like something's bothering you, Logan," Ari said gently.

Logan sighed. "It's James. He blew up at me over a stupid project. I didn't even say anything rude, but he took it all wrong. I just wanted to make our presentation accurate."

Ari tilted his head thoughtfully. "Conflict can be hard, especially when emotions get in the way. Do you think there's a way to handle this without making it worse?"

Logan thought about Ari's question. He realized that firing back at James wouldn't fix anything—it would only add more tension to their group. Maybe, instead of focusing on being right, he could try to see things from James's perspective.

The next day, Logan approached James before class. Taking a deep breath, he spoke calmly. "Hey, James, I wanted to say sorry if I came across as bossy. I didn't mean to sound like I know everything. I just thought it would be helpful if we double-checked our sources. Your ideas are important, too."

James looked surprised, and the tension in his face softened. "Uh… thanks, Logan. I guess I overreacted. I just didn't want my work to feel dismissed."

Logan smiled, relieved. "I get it. Maybe we can work together to find a balance so we both feel good about it?"

To Logan's surprise, James nodded, and they worked together to improve the project. What started as a disagreement turned into a moment of growth, all because Logan chose kindness

Afterward, Logan shared what happened with Ari, who nodded approvingly. "Kindness doesn't mean letting others walk all over you, Logan. It means approaching situations with empathy and choosing to listen rather than react. True strength lies in handling conflict with grace."

Logan realized that he felt proud—not just of the project, but of himself. By choosing kindness, he had built a bridge rather than a wall, and in doing so, he'd earned James's respect.

1. Have you ever faced a conflict where you felt misunderstood? How did you respond?

2. What are some ways you can choose kindness, even in tough situations?

3. How does handling conflict with empathy and kindness make you feel?

Quote:
"Kindness is not a weakness; it's the strength to respond with understanding when anger feels easier."

Bible Verse:
"Blessed are the peacemakers, for they will be called children of God." –
Matthew 5:9

You're truly gifted.

You're full of purpose.

CHAPTER 12

The Loss

Logan was at home, flipping through his messages, when he noticed an unusual number of missed calls and texts from friends. Confused, he opened one of the messages, and his heart dropped as he read the words: "Ethan passed away last night."

Ethan, his closest friend since they were kids—the one who always lit up every room and made Logan laugh like no one else. It didn't make sense. As he scrolled further, the truth hit harder. Ethan had struggled with things Logan never fully understood. The details were blurred, but the word "overdose" burned into his mind, leaving him numb and shattered.

The following days were a blur. Logan felt a storm of guilt, anger, sadness, and disbelief all at once. He couldn't shake the thought: How didn't I see this coming? Memories of Ethan's smile, his jokes, the dreams they shared, all replayed in his mind, now tinged with a heartbreaking finality.

One evening, Logan sat alone in his room, lost in the memories, when he felt the familiar warmth by his side. He looked up to see Ari, his lion guide, sitting close, his gentle eyes full of understanding.

"Why did this happen, Ari?" Logan whispered, his voice choked with pain. "How could he be gone just like that?"

Ari sat quietly, letting Logan's words settle before responding. "Sometimes, even the brightest lights carry heavy shadows, Logan. We can't always see the burdens others carry, no matter how close they are to us."

Logan swallowed hard, feeling the weight of regret. "But… he was my best friend. How could I not have known he was struggling?"

Ari placed a reassuring paw on Logan's shoulder. "There are battles that people fight in silence, battles they feel they can't share. Ethan's struggle doesn't reflect a lack of friendship—it reflects the complexity of being human. We often wear masks, even to those we love most."

Logan took a deep breath, tears welling up in his eyes. "I keep thinking of things I could have done differently… ways I could have been there for him."

Ari's gaze was steady, compassionate. "It's natural to feel that way. But remember, Logan, love isn't just in what we do; it's in who we are with others. Ethan knew you cared. He felt your friendship, your laughter, your support. Sometimes, that love is the brightest thing in a dark world, even if it doesn't change the outcome."

Logan wiped his eyes, nodding slowly. "I wish he'd just told me. I wish he'd trusted me enough to let me help."

Ari looked at him with wisdom that ran deep. "Perhaps part of honoring Ethan is to carry forward what you've learned. When we face loss, it teaches us to hold those we love a little closer, to check in a little more, and to walk more gently through life, knowing everyone has unseen struggles."

A few days later, Logan sat by himself in the park, watching the sunset. The world was peaceful, oblivious to the storm that had raged within him since Ethan's passing. As he sat there, he remembered Ari's words about honoring Ethan through the lessons he'd left behind.

He thought about the times they had laughed, the dreams they'd shared, and the unspoken understanding they'd had. He realized that Ethan's life, though shorter than he wished, had left a deep impact on him. Ethan had taught him about friendship, about being present, and about embracing life—even the moments that felt confusing or messy.

As the sun dipped below the horizon, Logan closed his eyes, whispering a silent promise to himself. I'll carry your light forward, Ethan. I'll look for those who might need a friend, and I'll remind myself every day that kindness can be the greatest gift.

In that quiet moment, he felt a shift. The sadness was still there, but it was softer now, less a wound and more a part of him. He would miss Ethan, and he would always wish he could have done more. But he also knew that Ethan's memory would inspire him to live with compassion, to listen more, to be there for others—and, most of all, to carry forward the friendship they had shared.

1. Practice Empathy:

Remember that people often fight silent battles. Be mindful and compassionate toward others, even if they seem okay on the surface. Everyone has struggles we may not see.

2. Cherish Your Connections:

True friendship means showing up, even in small ways. Let the people you care about know they're valued and loved. A simple check-in or listening ear can make all the difference.

3. Transform Pain into Purpose:

Loss and disappointment can inspire us to grow. Instead of dwelling on what you could have done differently, focus on what you can do now to honor those you've loved. Use the lessons learned to be a source of kindness and strength for others.

Quote:
"Grief is the price we pay for love." — Queen Elizabeth II

Bible Verse:
"The Lord is close to the brokenhearted and saves those who are crushed in spirit." — Psalm 34:18

You're potential is endless.

Keep your vision clear.

CHAPTER 13

The Pressure of Expectations

The following week at school felt different for Logan. After what happened at the park, he couldn't shake the feeling that something had shifted between him and his friends. He wasn't sure if it was because he hadn't gone along with the drinking, or if it was just in his head, but everything felt a little off.

At lunch, Logan sat with Daniel and the rest of their group, but he found himself feeling distant, like he didn't quite fit in anymore. The conversation shifted from weekend plans to an upcoming project for their history class, and before Logan knew it, the pressure was back.

"So, we're all meeting up at my house to work on the project this weekend," one of their friends, Lucas, said casually. "We'll get it done, and then we can hang out afterward."

Logan nodded along, but the truth was, he already knew his weekend would be packed. His parents had planned a family dinner, and he had a ton of homework to catch up on. But as Lucas and the others kept talking, Logan felt that familiar pull—the need to say yes, even though he knew it wasn't realistic.

"You're coming, right, Logan?" Lucas asked, raising an eyebrow.

Logan hesitated. "I don't know… I've got a lot of stuff going on this weekend."

Lucas smirked. "Come on, man. You've been missing out on a lot lately. Just ditch the family stuff for one day. It's no big deal."

Logan felt the pressure building again, the same way it had at the park. He didn't want to let his friends down, but he also didn't want to get caught up in something that would make his weekend even more stressful.

Ari, who had been sitting quietly under the table, sensed Logan's internal struggle. He nudged Logan's leg with his nose, his eyes full of understanding. "You don't have to agree to something just because they expect you to. Your time is important, too."

Logan glanced down at Ari, feeling a wave of guilt wash over him. He knew

Ari was right, but saying no felt impossible. If he backed out, he knew his friends would see him as the one who wasn't pulling his weight.

Before he could respond, Lucas leaned in. "What's the problem, man? It's just one afternoon. You don't want to be that guy who always bails out, do you?"

Logan's heart raced. He didn't want to be that guy—the one who always had an excuse, the one who couldn't keep up. But Ari's voice echoed in his mind, reminding him that he didn't have to be everything to everyone.

Taking a deep breath, Logan finally spoke. "I can't make it, Lucas. I've got family stuff going on, and I need to focus on that."

The table fell silent for a moment, and Logan could feel the weight of his friends' disappointment. Lucas raised an eyebrow, clearly surprised. "Alright, man. Whatever you say."

Daniel glanced over at Logan, his expression unreadable, but he didn't say anything. The rest of the group went back to their conversation, and Logan felt the sting of being left out once again.

That afternoon, Logan walked home with Daniel, the silence between them heavier than usual.

"You okay?" Daniel asked, breaking the quiet.

Logan nodded, but he didn't feel okay. "I just hate feeling like I'm letting everyone down, you know?"

Daniel gave a small shrug. "You didn't let anyone down. You've got your own stuff going on. It's not a crime to say no sometimes."

Logan looked at his friend, surprised by his response. "Yeah, but it still feels like… I don't know, like I'm not doing enough. Like I'm not part of the group anymore."

Daniel stopped walking and turned to face Logan. "Dude, you don't have to say yes to everything just to be part of the group. We're still your friends, even if you don't come to every hangout or every project session."

Ari, who had been quietly listening, spoke up. "It's easy to get caught up in what other people expect from you, but you've got to take care of yourself too. You can't be everywhere at once, Logan. And that's okay."

Logan sighed, feeling a little better but still unsure. "I guess I just don't want people to think I'm slacking off or that I don't care."

Daniel shook his head. "No one thinks that, man. And if they do, that's their problem, not yours."

Logan glanced down at Ari, who gave him an encouraging nod. "You're allowed to set boundaries, Logan. You don't have to please everyone."

As they continued walking, Logan felt the weight of the expectations slowly lift. It wasn't easy to say no, especially when everyone around him seemed to expect so much. But Ari's words stuck with him—he didn't have to meet every expectation. He didn't have to be perfect.

Meanwhile, Emma was dealing with her own form of peer pressure at school.

Her group of friends had been talking all week about a new fashion trend they'd seen on social media. The latest brand of sneakers had become an instant hit, and suddenly, everyone wanted a pair. Emma liked the shoes, sure, but they were expensive, and she knew her parents weren't going to shell out that kind of money for something that would be out of style in a few months.

Still, every day at school, more and more kids were showing up wearing the new sneakers, and Emma felt the pressure building. Her friends had already started dropping hints, asking her when she was going to get a pair. She'd laughed it off at first, but the more they talked about it, the more she felt like she was falling behind.

At lunch, one of her friends, Kayla, nudged her. "Hey, did you see Sarah's new sneakers? She got the limited edition ones. They're so cool!"

Emma smiled weakly. "Yeah, they're nice."

Kayla leaned in. "When are you getting yours? I heard the store's getting a new shipment next week."

Emma's stomach twisted. She hadn't told her friends that her parents weren't going to buy the sneakers for her. She didn't want to seem uncool or like she couldn't keep up with the trends, but the truth was, she didn't even care that much about the shoes. It was just the pressure to fit in that was making her feel like she needed them.

Ari, who had been sitting quietly beside Emma, spoke up. "You don't need those sneakers to be part of the group, Emma. You're enough just as you are."

Emma glanced down at Ari, feeling a sense of relief wash over her. He was right—she didn't need the sneakers to prove anything to anyone.

But before she could respond, Kayla nudged her again. "Come on, Em. You've got to get them. You don't want to be the only one without a pair, right?"

Emma swallowed hard, her heart racing. She didn't want to feel left out, but she also didn't want to give in to the pressure. Taking a deep breath, she finally spoke. "I'm not getting the sneakers, Kayla. They're too expensive, and I don't really need them."

Kayla looked surprised but didn't push it. "Oh… okay."

Ari smiled up at Emma, his presence a reminder that it was okay to stand your ground. "You don't need to follow the crowd, Emma. You're enough, with or without those shoes."

Emma smiled back at him, feeling a sense of pride in her decision. It wasn't easy to go against the pressure, but Ari had reminded her that her value wasn't tied to what she wore or what she owned.

Reflection Questions:

1. As with Logan, what external expectations in your life impact your self-image and your ability to handle challenges?

• How do these pressures affect how you approach your goals and responsibilities?

2. Ari says that true strength comes from rising again after falling. How do you define resilience in your own life?

3. What steps can you take to remind yourself that failure is not the end, but an opportunity to grow?

Quote:
"Our greatest glory is not in never falling, but in rising every time we fall."
– Confucius

Bible Verse:
"But they who wait for the Lord shall renew their strength; they shall mount up with wings like eagles; they shall run and not be weary; they shall walk and not faint." – Isaiah 40:31

You're a true warrior.

You're on the right path.

CHAPTER 14

The Power of Your Choices

It was a rainy Tuesday afternoon, and Logan was sitting at his desk, staring blankly at his math homework. The numbers on the page seemed to blur together, and the frustration was building with every minute that passed. No matter how hard he tried to focus, he just couldn't get it right.

"Why does this have to be so hard?" Logan muttered under his breath, pushing his notebook away in frustration.

Ari, who had been lying quietly at the foot of Logan's bed, lifted his head. He could sense the rising tension in Logan's voice, the familiar frustration that often came when things didn't go as planned.

"Having trouble with math again?" Ari asked gently, padding over to Logan's desk.

Logan ran a hand through his hair, sighing heavily. "It's not just math. It's everything. School, sports, trying to keep up with friends… It feels like no matter what I do, I'm just not good enough."

Ari sat beside him, his eyes full of understanding. "It's okay to feel frustrated, Logan. But giving up now won't help you get where you want to be."

Logan slumped back in his chair, his mind racing with doubts. "But what if I'm not meant for this? What if I'm just not smart enough or good enough to keep up with everything?"

Ari tilted his head, his gaze steady. "You know, it's not about being the best at everything. It's about not giving up when things get tough. Resilience isn't about never failing—it's about picking yourself up when you do."

Logan frowned, his frustration still simmering. "But what's the point if I keep failing anyway? Why keep trying if I'm just going to mess up?"

Ari nudged his leg gently. "Because every time you try, you're getting stronger. Every mistake you make is helping you learn. But if you give up now, you're stopping yourself from seeing how far you can go."

Logan looked down at the math problems in front of him, his mind spinning with thoughts of failure. He'd been struggling with this unit for weeks, and every time he thought he was making progress, he'd hit a wall. The more he tried, the more it felt like he was getting nowhere.

"It's just… hard," Logan admitted quietly. "I feel like I'm always falling behind. And sometimes, it feels easier to just… quit."

Ari's expression softened. "I know it's hard. But you're stronger than you think. You don't have to have it all figured out today. You just have to keep going, one step at a time."

Logan sighed again, but this time, the frustration seemed to ease a little. "What if I can't do it?"

Ari smiled gently. "You can. And if you stumble, that's okay. You're allowed to struggle. But every time you keep trying, you're building something important—resilience."

Logan sat in silence for a moment, thinking about Ari's words. Resilience. He'd heard that word before, but he hadn't really thought about what it meant for him. He'd always seen failure as something to avoid, something that meant he wasn't good enough. But maybe… maybe failing was just part of the process. Maybe it wasn't about always succeeding, but about having the strength to keep trying, even when things felt impossible.

The next day at school, Emma was having her own battle with resilience.

Gym class had never been her favorite. She wasn't the most athletic, and she often felt out of place compared to the girls who seemed to excel at every sport they tried. Today, they were running laps outside on the track, and Emma could feel herself falling behind, her legs burning with every step.

"Come on, Emma, you're almost there!" one of the gym teachers called out, but it felt like nothing more than background noise to her.

The other girls had already finished their laps, and Emma could feel the embarrassment rising in her chest. She wanted to stop, to just give up and sit on the sidelines, but something inside her told her to keep going.

Ari appeared at the edge of the track, his golden eyes watching her closely. "You're doing great, Emma. Keep going."

Emma shook her head, her breath coming in shallow gasps. "I'm so far behind, Ari. What's the point? Everyone else is already done."

Ari walked alongside her, his voice calm but firm. "It's not about finishing first. It's about not giving up. Every step you take is getting you closer. Don't stop now."

Emma wanted to argue, to tell Ari that she couldn't do it, that she wasn't strong enough. But as she looked at him, she realized something: Ari wasn't focused on how fast she was going or how far behind she was. He was focused on the fact that she was still moving forward.

"You're not in competition with anyone else, Emma," Ari said, his voice steady. "You're building your own strength, and that's what matters. Resilience is about pushing through, even when it feels hard."

Emma felt her legs burning, her breath ragged, but she kept going. She wasn't running to win anymore—she was running to prove to herself that she could. And as she crossed the finish line, long after the others had finished, she felt a sense of pride that had nothing to do with how fast she'd run.

"See?" Ari said, smiling up at her. "You didn't give up. And that's what makes you strong."

Emma collapsed onto the grass, exhausted but smiling. "It felt impossible."

Ari lay down beside her, his tail flicking playfully. "But you did it anyway. And that's what resilience is—doing the hard things, even when they feel impossible."

Back at home, Logan sat at his desk once again, his math homework spread out in front of him.

He still wasn't sure he'd get it right. He still wasn't sure he had what it took. But as he picked up his pencil and started working through the problems, he remembered what Ari had said.

Resilience wasn't about always getting it right. It was about not giving up when things went wrong.

And so, Logan kept going. Mistake after mistake, problem after problem. But this time, he didn't let the frustration stop (or even bother) him. He knew that every time he kept trying, he was getting stronger.

And that was enough.

Reflection Questions:

1. How do the choices you make reflect who you are and what you value?

2. How can you learn to make decisions based on what's right for you, not what others expect of you?

3. What choices are you currently facing that feel difficult? How can you approach them with wisdom?

Quote:
"We are our choices." – Jean-Paul Sartre

Bible Verse:
"For I have chosen him, so that he will direct his children and his household after him to keep the way of the Lord by doing what is right and just." –
Genesis 18:19

Stay inspired today.

Believe in your dreams.

CHAPTER 15

Embracing Change

It had been a tense couple of weeks at home, and Logan felt like he was constantly walking on eggshells. His parents had been fighting a lot lately—loud arguments that spilled into the late hours of the night, even when they thought he couldn't hear. But he could. He heard every word.

Logan sat at the kitchen table, staring at the untouched breakfast in front of him. His mom was busy getting ready for work, while his dad sat across from him, silently reading the news on his phone. The air between them was thick with unspoken words, and it made Logan's stomach twist.

Ari sat beside him, his presence quiet but steady, as always. He could feel the tension in the room, too.

"Are you okay?" Ari asked softly, his golden eyes full of concern.

Logan didn't respond at first, unsure of how to put what he was feeling into words. The truth was, he wasn't okay. His parents hadn't told him directly yet, but he knew something was wrong. The constant fighting, the way they avoided each other's eyes—it was like everything was falling apart.

Finally, Logan spoke, his voice barely above a whisper. "I don't know."

Ari sat closer, offering comfort in the silence. "It's okay not to know right now."

The sound of the front door closing snapped Logan out of his thoughts. His mom had already left for work without saying goodbye, and his dad stood up, grabbing his keys.

"I'll be home late tonight," his dad said, barely glancing in Logan's direction. "You okay here?"

Logan nodded, but inside, he felt like screaming. He wasn't okay. Nothing was okay.

As his dad left, Logan sat alone in the kitchen, the quietness of the house settling around him like a heavy blanket. He didn't understand how everything had gone so wrong. Just a few months ago, things had been normal. Sure, his parents argued sometimes, but it was never like this. Now, it was like they couldn't even be in the same room without fighting.

Ari nudged Logan's leg gently. "You don't have to keep it all inside, you know."

Logan looked down at Ari, tears welling up in his eyes. "But what am I supposed to do? I feel like… like everything's falling apart, and no one's telling me anything."

Ari's eyes softened. "It's hard when the people you look up to for stability are the ones who seem the most unstable. But you don't have to carry it all on your own."

Logan wiped his eyes with the back of his hand. "I just… I don't know how to handle this. I don't even know if they're going to stay together."

Ari sat quietly for a moment before speaking. "No matter what happens between them, you're not alone. Their decisions don't define who you are, and whatever they're going through, it's not your fault."

Logan nodded, but the words felt heavy. "It feels like it is, though. Like maybe if I were better, or if I didn't make things so hard for them, they wouldn't be fighting all the time."

Ari stood up and put his paw on Logan's knee, his voice gentle but firm. "This isn't because of you. People go through hard things, and sometimes they don't know how to fix them. But it doesn't mean you did anything wrong."

Logan took a deep breath, trying to steady himself. He knew Ari was right, but the guilt was still there, gnawing at him. How could he not feel responsible when his whole world was falling apart around him?

Later that evening, Logan sat in his room, staring blankly at his phone.

The news had finally come. His parents had sat him down after dinner and told him they were getting a divorce. It wasn't a long conversation—his dad had done most of the talking, while his mom sat quietly, her face pale and tired. They said all the things Logan had heard before from other kids going through the same thing: "This isn't your fault," "We still love you," "We just can't make it work anymore."

But none of it made him feel any better. The truth was, their words felt empty, like promises that had already been broken.

Logan's phone buzzed with a message from Daniel, but he ignored it. He didn't want to talk to anyone right now. Not even his friends. What was he supposed to say? That his life was falling apart? That his parents were getting a divorce and he didn't know how to deal with it?

Ari hopped onto the bed beside him, curling up next to Logan's side. "It's okay to feel angry, you know. Or sad. Or confused. You don't have to hold it all together."

Logan stared at the ceiling, blinking back tears. "I just… I thought they'd figure it out, you know? I didn't think it would come to this."

Ari rested his head on Logan's chest, his presence grounding. "Sometimes people can't fix things, even when they want to. It's not fair, but that doesn't mean you have to go through this alone."

Logan swallowed hard, trying to keep his emotions in check. "But what now? What's supposed to happen next?"

Ari looked up at him, his golden eyes filled with empathy. "Now, you take it one day at a time. You don't have to have all the answers right now. It's okay to feel lost, to feel hurt. But you're stronger than you think, Logan. And no matter what happens with your parents, you'll find your way through this."

Logan closed his eyes, letting the tears fall. He didn't have to be strong right now. He didn't have to have it all figured out. And for the first time in weeks, he let himself feel the sadness, the confusion, the anger—everything he'd been holding inside.

Ari stayed by his side, a quiet reminder that even when things felt like they were falling apart, he wasn't alone. He didn't have to carry the weight of his parents' divorce on his own. And even though the road ahead felt uncertain, he knew that somehow, he would get through it.

Reflection Questions:

1. Have you ever felt the pressure to follow someone else's path? How did that make you feel?

2. What helps you trust your own journey, even when it doesn't look like anyone else's?

3. How can you embrace the idea that everyone's path is different, and that's okay?

Quote:
"Your path is your path. Don't let someone else's path distract you from your journey." – Unknown

Bible Verse:
"Trust in the Lord with all your heart and lean not on your own understanding; in all your ways submit to him, and he will make your paths straight." – Proverbs 3:5-6

You're making progress.

You're full of purpose.

CHAPTER 16

Beyond the Familiar

It started in the most unexpected way—a simple Sunday morning at church. Logan had been feeling lost after his parents' divorce, and church was the one place where everything felt a little quieter. A little more peaceful. It wasn't that Logan was deeply religious, but there was something about being there, sitting in the pews, that gave him a sense of comfort he couldn't find anywhere else.

That morning, the pastor talked about an upcoming mission trip. A group from the church was traveling to the Philippines to help build a church in a rural village. As Logan listened to the announcement, something stirred inside him—a curiosity, maybe even a calling. He'd never been on a mission trip before, let alone to a place like the Philippines, but for some reason, the idea wouldn't leave his mind.

After the service, Logan found himself signing up for the trip, almost on autopilot. He didn't know what he was looking for, but something inside him felt like he needed to be part of this.

A few weeks later, Logan was on a plane, bound for a country he knew almost nothing about.

As the plane touched down in Manila, the capital of the Philippines, Logan peered out the window, trying to take in the unfamiliar sights. The city was busy, alive with the sounds of honking cars and people rushing about their day. It was nothing like home.

From Manila, the mission group took a long bus ride to a small village far from the hustle of the city. The roads were rough, and the heat was intense, but the people they met along the way greeted them with warm smiles and waves. Logan noticed something right away—everyone seemed happy. There was a lightness in their faces, a joy that didn't seem tied to anything material.

When they arrived at the village, Logan expected to feel overwhelmed by the differences—the simple homes made of bamboo and thatch, the lack of electricity in some parts, the basic lifestyle. But instead, he was greeted with something else: laughter.

The kids in the village ran up to greet the mission team, giggling and telling silly jokes that Logan didn't fully understand but couldn't help laughing at anyway. The adults welcomed them with open arms, and the atmosphere was filled with song. Everywhere Logan turned, someone was singing—while working, while walking, while playing.

Logan couldn't help but notice how different it was from back home. At home, people seemed to need everything—new clothes, the latest gadgets, fancy cars—to feel happy. Here, in this small village with so little, the people seemed happier than anyone Logan had ever known.

As the days passed, Logan got to work with the rest of the mission group, helping to build the new church.

It was hard labor—mixing cement, carrying bricks, hammering nails—but there was something fulfilling about it. Every day, the villagers worked alongside the mission group, singing and laughing as they went. Even in the heat of the day, when Logan was drenched in sweat and ready to collapse, the Filipinos around him kept going, their spirits unbreakable.

One afternoon, during a break, Logan sat down with a few of the kids from the village. They didn't speak much English, but they communicated through smiles, hand gestures, and a few basic words they'd picked up from the mission team.

One of the kids, a boy named Carlo, sat beside Logan, humming a song as he played with a small stick. Logan smiled at him, impressed by the boy's carefree attitude.

"You like to sing, huh?" Logan asked, even though he wasn't sure if Carlo understood.

Carlo nodded enthusiastically and began to hum louder, a big grin spreading across his face.

"Do you like to sing because it makes you happy?" Logan asked.

Carlo stopped humming for a moment and looked at Logan, his eyes twinkling. "Sing… makes… heart happy," he said in broken English, tapping his chest.

Logan smiled, feeling a warmth spread through him. He hadn't thought much about singing before—at least, not like this. But here, in this village, it was like singing was a language of its own, a way to express joy and gratitude that didn't rely on having anything material.

That evening, Logan sat outside under the stars with Ari beside him, reflecting on what he'd seen and felt over the past few days.

It's crazy," Logan said softly, running his hand through Ari's fur. "These people… they don't have anything like what we have back home. No big houses, no fancy cars. But they're happy. Like, really happy. There's joy everywhere I turned, and it's not because of stuff, it's because of… I don't know, something else. Something real."

Ari looked up at Logan, his golden eyes full of wisdom. "Happiness doesn't come from the things we own, Logan. It comes from the way we choose to live."

Logan nodded, thinking about the smiles, the laughter, the singing. "Yeah. I think I took a lot for granted back home. I thought you needed stuff to be happy. But here… they don't have much, and it doesn't even matter."

Ari smiled. "Sometimes it takes seeing another way of life to understand what truly matters. The Filipinos you've met—they've found joy in community, in laughter, in music. They know that the most valuable things in life aren't things at all."

Logan sat quietly for a while, listening to the distant sound of someone singing in the village. The realization hit him hard. He had spent so much of his life thinking that happiness came from having more—more stuff, more success, more approval from others. But here, in a place where people had so little, he'd seen more joy than he ever had back home.

"I think… I needed this," Logan said quietly. "I needed to see that happiness isn't about what you have. It's about who you are and how you live."

Ari nodded. "That's a lesson some people never learn. But you're starting to understand it now."

Logan smiled to himself, feeling a sense of peace he hadn't felt in a long time. The trip to the Philippines had shown him something he couldn't have learned anywhere else. And as he sat under the stars, surrounded by the sounds of laughter and music, he knew that this experience had changed him.

Reflection Questions:

1. Have you ever experienced something that made you see life differently, like Logan did during his mission trip?

2. How can learning about other cultures and perspectives help you grow as a person?

3. How can you be more open to seeing the world through the eyes of others?

Quote:
"The real voyage of discovery consists not in seeking new landscapes, but in having new eyes." – Marcel Proust

Bible Verse:
"Do nothing out of selfish ambition or vain conceit. Rather, in humility value others above yourselves." – Philippians 2:3

You're a true warrior.

Embrace your journey.

CHAPTER 17

A Taste of New Adventures

After a long day of working on the new church, the mission group was tired but in good spirits. The foundation was nearly complete, and with every brick laid, they could see the project coming to life. As the sun began to set, casting a golden glow over the village, the group received an invitation they hadn't expected.

Pastor Manuel, the leader of the small Filipino church, had invited the entire mission team to his home for dinner. Logan had been looking forward to a quiet evening to unwind, but something about the invitation felt special. The pastor's warmth and kindness throughout their stay had already made an impression, so when he offered to host them, it felt like an invitation that couldn't be refused.

The mission group arrived at the pastor's modest home, where a long table had been set up in the open-air yard. As they approached, Logan's eyes widened at the sight before him. The table was overflowing with food—dishes of all shapes, colors, and aromas that he didn't recognize. The villagers had gone all out to welcome the mission group, and their joy was evident in the way they moved around the table, filling every plate with care and excitement.

Pastor Manuel greeted them with a wide smile, his hands outstretched. "Welcome! We are honored to share this meal with you. Everything here was prepared with love by our community."

Logan smiled back, but inside, he felt a flicker of hesitation. The food looked and smelled… different. He had never seen dishes like these before. There were meats marinated in sauces he couldn't identify, bowls of unfamiliar vegetables, and rice served in what looked like banana leaves. It wasn't anything like the food he was used to back home.

The mission group began to gather around the table, and Logan's stomach growled, reminding him of how hungry he was. But as he looked at the spread before him, uncertainty gnawed at him. What if I don't like it? he thought. What if I can't eat it?

Ari, ever by his side, nudged Logan's leg gently. "You're worried about the food, aren't you?"

Logan glanced down at Ari, his expression uneasy. "Yeah… I mean, I don't want to be rude, but I don't know what any of this is. What if I can't eat it?"

Ari's golden eyes sparkled with understanding. "It's okay to be unsure, Logan. But remember, this food was made with love and joy. Sometimes, trying new things isn't just about the food—it's about being open to the experience and showing respect for the people who've welcomed you."

Logan nodded slowly, watching as Pastor Manuel and the others began to serve the dishes, laughing and talking as they passed plates around the table. The atmosphere was so warm, so filled with gratitude and happiness, that Logan couldn't help but feel the weight of his hesitation begin to lift.

Pastor Manuel approached with a plate, offering it to Logan with a smile. "This is one of our favorite dishes—adobo," he said, gesturing to the marinated meat. "Please, try it. It is a blessing to share this meal with you."

Logan hesitated for only a second before taking the plate. He could see the care in the pastor's eyes, the pride in what had been prepared. "Thank you," Logan said, his voice a little quieter than usual. He took a deep breath and put a small bite of the adobo into his mouth.

To his surprise, the flavors were rich and comforting. The meat was tender, cooked in a tangy, savory sauce that was unlike anything he'd tasted before— but in a good way.

Ari smiled beside him. "See? It's not so bad, is it?"

Logan grinned, realizing how silly he had been to hesitate. "No, it's actually really good."

As the night went on, Logan tried more dishes—pancit, a noodle dish bursting with flavor; lumpia, crispy spring rolls stuffed with vegetables and meat; and halo-halo, a colorful dessert made with shaved ice, fruits, and sweet beans. Every bite was a new experience, and with each dish, Logan's initial hesitation melted away, replaced by a deep sense of gratitude.

He watched the villagers as they laughed and shared stories, their smiles wide and genuine. Despite having so little in terms of material wealth, they were rich in ways that truly mattered—in joy, in love, and in community. And now, they were sharing all of that with Logan and his mission group.

By the end of the meal, Logan felt more than full. He felt satisfied in a way that went beyond the food. It wasn't just about the dishes they had shared— it was about the connection he felt with these people. The pastor's invitation had been more than a simple meal; it had been a reminder to be open, flexible, and respectful of new experiences, no matter how unfamiliar they might seem at first.

As the night drew to a close and the mission group prepared to leave, Pastor Manuel placed a hand on Logan's shoulder. "Thank you for being part of this," he said. "I know it may have been different from what you're used to, but it means so much to us that you shared this meal with us."

Logan smiled, feeling a deep sense of gratitude. "Thank you for inviting us. This… this was really special."

As they walked back to the mission house, Logan turned to Ari, his heart full. "You were right, Ari. I didn't realize how much I needed this. I was so focused on what was different that I almost missed out on something amazing."

Ari nodded. "Sometimes the best experiences come when we let go of our fears and open ourselves to the unknown. You showed respect by trying something new, and in doing so, you found something greater than what you expected."

Logan looked up at the stars, feeling a sense of peace he hadn't felt in a long time. He had learned something important that night—that being open, flexible, and respectful could lead to the most fulfilling experiences. And as he reflected on the joy and gratitude of the people around him, he realized that maybe, just maybe, he was starting to understand what truly mattered in life.

Reflection Questions:

1. Have you ever tried something new that you were hesitant about, like Logan with the unfamiliar food? How did it change your perspective?

2. How can you be more open to new experiences, even when they feel uncomfortable?

3. What "new beginnings" are you facing in your life right now? How can you approach them with an open heart?

Quote:
"Every moment is a fresh beginning." – T.S. Eliot

Bible Verse:
"See, I am doing a new thing! Now it springs up; do you not perceive it? I am making a way in the wilderness and streams in the wasteland." – Isaiah 43:19

Great things await you.

CHAPTER 18

Reflections from the Sky

Logan sat in the window seat of the airplane, gazing out at the clouds as they floated by. The mission trip to the Philippines had changed him in ways he hadn't expected. He had come to help build a church, but was leaving with a heart full of gratitude and reflection, moved by the experiences and connections he had made.

The flight was long, giving Logan plenty of time to think. He couldn't stop replaying the images of the people he had met—especially the kids. The joy in their faces, their laughter, their endless energy, even though they didn't have much. He remembered the beggars on the streets of Manila, some of them smiling as they held out their hands, asking for food. How could they smile like that, when they had so little?

And then there were the kids in the village who couldn't go to school. He had asked Pastor Manuel about it, curious as to why so many of the children were out playing during the day instead of attending classes.

"Some of them can't afford school," the pastor had explained. "It's not free like it is in other countries. Some families have to choose between sending their kids to school or putting food on the table."

That conversation had stuck with Logan. Back in America, school was a given. It wasn't something he'd ever had to think about—just something you did, whether you liked it or not. But in the Philippines, education was a privilege, not a guarantee. Logan couldn't shake the sadness that came with knowing how different life was depending on where you were born.

By the time the plane landed in the U.S., Logan felt a strange mix of emotions.

As he stepped out into the airport, he was greeted by the familiar sights and sounds of home—the bustling crowds, the polished floors, the convenience of everything. His parents were there waiting for him, smiling and waving, though their relationship still felt distant, like something that had been patched up but never quite healed.

Over the next few days, that feeling didn't go away. Logan went back to his normal routine, but everything felt… off. He walked through the halls of his high school, noticing how much everyone had—new clothes, expensive shoes, backpacks loaded with all the latest gadgets. Everything seemed so easy, so plentiful. And yet, all he could think about were the kids in the Philippines who didn't have these things but still smiled. Who found joy in the smallest of moments, even when they didn't know where their next meal was coming from.

At lunch, Logan sat with Daniel and their friends, but he couldn't keep up with the conversation. They were talking about the latest video games and plans for the weekend, but Logan's mind was elsewhere. He was thinking about the family he'd met in the village, whose house had only two small rooms for seven people. About the boy he'd seen on the streets of Manila, begging for food in the scorching heat, but still offering a shy smile when someone passed by.

Daniel nudged him. "Hey, you okay? You've been pretty quiet since you got back."

Logan looked up, realizing he hadn't said a word in nearly half an hour. "Yeah… I guess I'm just thinking."

Daniel raised an eyebrow. "About what?"

Logan hesitated, unsure how to explain the heaviness in his heart. "It's just… after being in the Philippines, everything here feels so different. I saw people who didn't have anything—beggars on the streets, kids who can't go to school because their parents can't afford it. But they were still happy. They still smiled. And then I come back here, and we have… everything. And it just feels unfair, you know?"

Daniel nodded slowly, trying to understand. "Yeah, I get that. It's hard to wrap your head around stuff like that."

Logan sighed, running a hand through his hair. "I just… I don't get it. How can life be so different depending on where you're born? How can people have so little and still be happy, while we have so much and don't even appreciate it?"

Ari, sitting quietly at Logan's side, finally spoke. "It's a hard thing to understand, Logan. The world isn't fair, and sometimes it feels overwhelming when you see that kind of disparity. But what matters is what you do with what you've learned."

Logan nodded, but the sadness didn't leave him. "I know. I just feel… guilty, I guess. Guilty that I've taken so much for granted."

Ari looked up at him, his golden eyes full of wisdom. "It's okay to feel that way. But remember, guilt won't change anything. What will make a difference is how you carry this experience forward. You've seen a different way of life, and now you have the chance to live with more gratitude, more awareness, and more compassion."

Logan sat in silence for a moment, thinking about Ari's words. He knew he couldn't change the world, but maybe he could change the way he lived in it. Maybe he could do more to help, even if it was just in small ways. And maybe, just maybe, he could find a way to share the joy he'd seen in the Philippines with the people around him.

That evening, Logan sat with his parents at the dinner table, the usual spread of food laid out before them.

The meal was simple by American standards, but to Logan, it felt like a feast compared to what he had seen in the Philippines. He thought about the families he'd met, the ones who shared what little they had with so much gratitude. And here he was, surrounded by abundance.

His mom noticed his silence. "How are you feeling, Logan? You've been pretty quiet since you got back."

Logan took a deep breath, unsure of how to explain what he was feeling. "It's just… after seeing how people live in the Philippines, I guess it's hard to come back and not feel like… we take so much for granted."

His dad nodded, his expression thoughtful. "I can imagine. It must've been eye-opening."

"It was," Logan said quietly. "I saw kids who can't go to school because their parents can't afford it. Beggars who didn't have enough to eat but still smiled. And I just keep thinking about how different it is here. We have so much, and we don't even realize it."

His mom reached across the table and placed a hand on his. "It's good that you see that, Logan. It means you're growing. And maybe now that you've seen how things are in other parts of the world, you can find ways to help, even from here."

Logan looked up at her, feeling a small sense of comfort. "Yeah. I want to do something. I don't know what yet, but I can't just go back to how things were."

Ari, sitting by the kitchen door, smiled quietly. "That's the beginning of change, Logan. When you start to see the world with new eyes, it changes you. And that change? That's where compassion grows."

Logan smiled to himself, feeling a sense of peace he hadn't experienced in a long time. The trip to the Philippines had taught him something he could never have learned anywhere else. As he sat under the stars, surrounded by laughter and music, he realized this experience had changed something deep inside him.

1. Have you ever witnessed something that made you see life differently? How did it change your perspective?

2. How do you think you can show more gratitude for the things you often take for granted?

3. Logan felt a sense of guilt for having more than others. How can we turn feelings of guilt into positive actions to help others?

4. What can you do in your daily life to carry forward the compassion Logan discovered on his trip?

Quote:
"Do what you can, with what you have, where you are." – Theodore Roosevelt

Bible Verse:
"Let each of you look not only to his own interests, but also to the interests of others." – Philippians 2:4

You are valued.

Your courage radiates.

CHAPTER 19

Standing Tall

It started with a few snickers and whispers. Logan hadn't thought much of it at first—just some comments here and there about him leaving early on Sunday mornings for church. But over time, the teasing became more pointed.

"Hey, Logan, where's your Bible? You gonna preach to us?" one of the guys from his math class, Tyler, sneered as they walked through the hallway after school.

Logan ignored the comment and kept walking, but the pit in his stomach grew. It wasn't the first time he'd heard it, and he knew it wouldn't be the last. Ever since he had returned from his mission trip to the Philippines, Logan had been more open about his faith, more committed to attending church, and even participating in youth group. He felt like the trip had changed him, but not everyone saw it that way.

Tyler and his friends had started teasing him about it a few weeks ago, at first just making small jokes, but now it seemed like they were looking for any opportunity to mock him.

As Logan walked out of the school and toward the bus stop, he felt a tap on his shoulder. It was Daniel, his best friend, who had noticed the exchange in the hallway.

"You okay, man?" Daniel asked, his face filled with concern.

Logan shrugged, trying to brush it off. "Yeah, I'm fine. Just… tired of hearing it, you know?"

Daniel nodded. "They're just messing with you. Don't let it get to you."

Logan let out a sigh as they waited for the bus. "It's just annoying. Like, why does it matter to them that I go to church? It's not like I'm preaching to them or anything."

Ari, who had been walking quietly beside Logan, spoke up. "Sometimes people tease what they don't understand, Logan. It's easier for them to mock something different than to try and understand it."

Logan looked down at Ari, his mind swirling with frustration. "I guess. But it doesn't make it any easier."

The teasing continued over the next few days.

At lunch, Tyler and his group made a habit of mocking Logan whenever they could. "Hey, Logan, you going to pray over your pizza?" one of them called out, laughing.

Logan clenched his fists under the table, doing his best to ignore them. But inside, the words stung. He didn't understand why they cared so much about his faith. Why was it such a big deal to them that he went to church?

Later that day, Logan found himself sitting alone on the bleachers after school, trying to clear his mind. Ari sat beside him, sensing his inner turmoil.

"You're frustrated," Ari said softly, his eyes full of empathy.

Logan nodded, staring out at the empty field. "Yeah, I am. It's like no matter what I do, they're always going to make fun of me. And the worst part is… sometimes I wonder if it would just be easier to stop going. To stop talking about it."

Ari tilted his head, watching Logan closely. "Would that make you feel better?"

Logan hesitated, his heart heavy with the question. "I don't know. I don't think so. But it would definitely make things easier."

Ari nudged Logan gently. "But easier isn't always better. You've found something in your faith that gives you strength, that gives you peace. Don't let a few people's opinions take that away from you."

Logan sighed, knowing Ari was right. But it didn't make the teasing any easier to handle. He had always been someone who tried to avoid conflict, someone who didn't like standing out too much. And now, because of his faith, he felt like he had a target on his back.

The next day, things came to a head.

Logan was at his locker when Tyler and his friends approached, smirking as they leaned against the lockers next to his.

"So, Logan," Tyler began, crossing his arms. "You heading to church again this weekend? Gonna pray for all of us sinners, huh?"

Logan's jaw tightened. He wanted to fire back, to say something that would make them back off. But before he could, Tyler's friend, Matt, chimed in.

"Yeah, maybe you can pray for us to get better grades or something. Isn't that how it works?"

The group laughed, and Logan felt his face flush with frustration. He knew they were trying to get a rise out of him, to make him feel small. But something inside him stirred—a reminder of the lessons he had learned during his trip to the Philippines, the joy and gratitude he had seen in the people there, despite their hardships. He remembered the strength they had in their faith, and how they had taught him that standing firm in what you believe isn't always easy, but it's worth it.

Taking a deep breath, Logan turned to face them, his voice calm but steady. "You can say whatever you want, but it's not going to change what I believe. Yeah, I go to church. Yeah, I pray. And it's something that gives me peace. So, if you've got a problem with that, that's on you."

The laughter died down as Tyler and his friends exchanged surprised glances. They hadn't expected Logan to stand up for himself like that. For a moment, there was silence, and then Tyler shrugged, clearly unimpressed but not sure what else to say.

"Whatever, man," Tyler muttered, before walking away with his friends.

Logan let out a long breath, feeling a mixture of relief and nerves. Standing up for himself hadn't been easy, but it felt… good. He had spoken his truth, and that was what mattered.

Ari smiled up at him, his eyes full of pride. "You stood tall, Logan. And that's what counts. You don't have to hide who you are just because some people don't understand it."

Logan nodded, feeling a weight lift off his shoulders. "Yeah. I guess I just have to remember that what they think doesn't really matter."

"Exactly," Ari said, his tail wagging gently. "Your faith is part of who you are. Don't let anyone take that away from you."

As Logan walked home that day, he felt lighter, more at peace. The teasing might not stop right away, but now he knew how to handle it. He didn't have to hide who he was or what he believed. And even though it wasn't always easy, he knew that standing firm in his faith made him stronger.

1. Have you ever been teased or judged for something you believe in? How did it make you feel, and how did you respond?

2. Why do you think people make fun of things they don't understand? How can you respond in a way that is true to yourself?

3. What does "standing tall" mean to you? Can you think of a time when you had to stand up for your beliefs, even when it was difficult?

4. How can you find peace and strength in being different, like Logan did?

Quote:
"Stand for what is right, even if it means standing alone." – Unknown

Bible Verse:
"Be on your guard; stand firm in the faith; be courageous; be strong."
– 1 Corinthians 16:13

Keep pushing forward.

Embrace your uniqueness.

CHAPTER 20

Finding the Real You

Logan sat at his desk, scrolling through his phone, feeling more and more frustrated with every image that flashed across the screen. It seemed like everyone was perfect—perfect skin, perfect hair, perfect clothes. He couldn't help but compare himself to the people he saw online, wondering why he never seemed to measure up.

It wasn't just the influencers or celebrities, either. Even his classmates seemed to have it all together. On Instagram, everyone was posting their best versions of themselves—pictures of weekends at the beach, group shots from the latest party, selfies with flawless filters. It all felt so… fake, but at the same time, it was hard to ignore.

Logan sighed, tossing his phone onto the bed and leaning back in his chair. The pressure to look a certain way, to fit in with what everyone else was doing, felt suffocating sometimes. He didn't want to care, but somehow, it was always there—this nagging feeling that he wasn't enough.

Ari sat beside him, watching as Logan rubbed his eyes in frustration. "You've been staring at that screen for a while. What's going on?"

Logan groaned. "It's just… I don't get it. How come everyone looks so perfect? And why do I feel like I'm the only one who doesn't?"

Ari tilted his head, his eyes full of understanding. "Because social media shows you only what people want you to see. It's not real life, Logan. It's a snapshot, filtered and edited to look perfect. But underneath, everyone has the same insecurities."

Logan shook his head, leaning forward with his elbows on his knees. "It doesn't feel that way. It feels like I'm the only one who's still figuring things out. Like everyone else has it all together, and I'm just… me."

Ari walked over and sat beside Logan's chair, his voice calm but sure. "The world tells you that how you look is the most important thing. But it's not. You're more than what you see in the mirror. What really matters is who you are—how you treat others, how you live, and the choices you make."

Logan sat back, staring up at the ceiling. He knew Ari was right, but it was hard to ignore the pressure. It seemed like no matter what he did, there was always something to compare himself to.

"Yeah, but everyone cares about appearances," Logan muttered. "It's like if you don't look a certain way, you don't matter."

Ari's golden eyes softened. "What if I told you that everyone who looks perfect on the outside is struggling with something inside? What you see online doesn't show the whole story. People hide behind filters and photos because they feel the same insecurities you do."

Logan glanced at his phone, still lying on the bed. "I guess. But it doesn't make it easier to deal with."

Ari nodded. "I know. But remember, your value doesn't come from how you look. It comes from who you are—your kindness, your compassion, your courage. Those are the things that truly make you stand out."

Logan sighed, rubbing his hands over his face. He wanted to believe that. He wanted to stop caring so much about how he looked or how he compared to others. But the pressure was everywhere—at school, online, even in random conversations.

Later that week, the pressure hit harder than usual.

It was Friday, and everyone was talking about a big party happening that weekend. Logan had been invited, but as the day went on, he started to dread going. He knew that everyone would show up looking their best, posting pictures all over social media, and the thought of having to keep up with that made him feel… tired.

At lunch, Daniel noticed the tension on Logan's face. "You alright? You don't seem too excited about the party tomorrow."

Logan shrugged, pushing his food around his plate. "I don't know. I guess I'm just not feeling it."

Daniel raised an eyebrow. "Not feeling it? That's not like you. What's going on?"

Logan hesitated, not wanting to admit how much the whole thing was getting to him. "I just… I don't know. It's dumb, but it feels like there's all this pressure to look a certain way. Like, if you don't show up looking perfect, why even go?"

Daniel frowned, looking genuinely surprised. "Dude, no one's thinking about that. We're all just going to hang out. No one cares if you look like you stepped out of a magazine."

Logan shrugged again, but inside, he knew that wasn't entirely true. He had seen the pictures from previous parties—the group shots where everyone looked flawless, like they were living out some kind of perfect teen movie. He couldn't help but feel like he didn't belong in those moments, like he wasn't enough.

That night, as Logan got ready for bed, Ari sat beside him, watching as Logan moved around the room in silence.

"You know, the more you chase after what the world tells you is important, the emptier you'll feel," Ari said quietly. "No matter how perfect someone looks on the outside, it won't fill the gaps inside. You're already enough, Logan. You don't need to prove anything."

Logan sat on the edge of his bed, feeling the weight of Ari's words. "But it feels like I do. It feels like if I don't look a certain way, people won't notice me. Or worse, they'll notice, but for the wrong reasons."

Ari smiled gently. "People will always have opinions, but you don't have to live by them. What matters is how you see yourself. And if you can start to see yourself the way I see you, you'll realize that you're already more than enough."

Logan lay back on his bed, staring up at the ceiling. The pressure to look a certain way might not disappear overnight, but maybe—just maybe—he could start to let go of some of it. Maybe he could start to see himself the way Ari saw him: not for the clothes he wore or the way he looked, but for who he was inside.

And maybe, just maybe, that would be enough.

Reflection Questions:

1. Have you ever compared yourself to someone online or in real life? How did it make you feel?

2. Social media shows only the best parts of people's lives. How can you remind yourself that no one's life is perfect, no matter how it looks?

3. What qualities do you value most in yourself? How can you focus on those instead of trying to live up to others' expectations?

4. What does it mean to you to be "more than what you see in the mirror"?

Quote:
"Don't compare your behind-the-scenes with someone else's highlight reel."
– Steven Furtick

Bible Verse:
"You are altogether beautiful, my darling; there is no flaw in you." – Song of Solomon 4:7

Believe in your impact.

You're destined for greatness.

CHAPTER 21

Fearfully and Wonderfully Made

It was one of those nights where everything seemed too much. The weight of expectations, the pressures of school, friends, and the unspoken rules of how to fit in—it all felt overwhelming. Logan lay in bed, staring at the ceiling, his mind racing with thoughts he couldn't escape.

He rolled over and grabbed his phone, scrolling mindlessly through social media. Every post seemed to highlight something he didn't have—better clothes, cooler friends, more success. He couldn't help but wonder if he would ever measure up. The world seemed so focused on appearances, accomplishments, and perfection, and Logan felt like he was falling short in every category.

As he lay there, a thought flickered in the back of his mind—something he'd heard in church a long time ago. It was a verse from the Bible, one that had stuck with him, though he hadn't thought about it in a while. "I am fearfully and wonderfully made." The words echoed faintly, tugging at his heart.

Ari, sensing Logan's inner turmoil, appeared beside the bed, his presence calm and steady. "What's on your mind tonight, Logan?"

Logan sighed, setting his phone down. "I don't know. It's just… I keep wondering if I'm good enough. If I'll ever be good enough. Everyone seems to have it all figured out, and I feel like I'm just… lost."

Ari sat quietly for a moment before speaking. "Do you remember Psalm 139?"

Logan blinked, surprised by the question. "Yeah… I guess. It's the one about God knowing everything about you, right?"

Ari nodded. "Yes. It's about how deeply you are known, how every part of you was created with care. You are 'fearfully and wonderfully made,' Logan. There's nothing about you that was an accident."

Logan sat up, feeling a strange mixture of comfort and unease. "But it's hard to believe that sometimes. I mean, look at me. I mess up all the time. I don't feel like I'm fearfully and wonderfully made."

Ari smiled softly, his golden eyes full of understanding. "It's easy to believe the lies the world tells you—that you're only worth what you can accomplish or how you look. But the truth, Logan, is that you were known and loved before you were even born. Every part of you was crafted with intention."

Logan thought about that for a moment, the words slowly sinking in. "But why do I feel so… insignificant?"

Ari's voice was gentle but firm. "Because you've been looking at yourself through the eyes of the world, not through the eyes of the One who created you. Psalm 139 reminds you that God has searched you and known you—every thought, every fear, every dream. He knows you better than you know yourself, and still, you are loved beyond measure."

Logan closed his eyes, trying to absorb the weight of those words. "You know when I sit and when I rise," he whispered, remembering the psalm. "You perceive my thoughts from afar."

Ari nodded. "Exactly. There is nowhere you can go where God is not with you. Whether you're at your best or your worst, He is there, guiding you, loving you, reminding you of your worth."

Logan's heart began to lighten, the familiar feeling of inadequacy slowly fading. "I guess I forget that sometimes. I get so caught up in trying to be perfect that I forget I'm already loved for who I am."

Ari stood beside the bed, his presence comforting. "You are seen, Logan. Every part of you—the parts you're proud of and the parts you try to hide—are known. And still, you are wonderfully made."

The next day, Logan sat in church, the words of Psalm 139 echoing in his mind.

As the pastor spoke, Logan felt a quiet sense of peace settling over him. The pressures that had weighed him down so heavily the night before didn't seem as overwhelming now. He wasn't defined by his mistakes or by how well he fit in with others. His worth was rooted in something much deeper—in the truth that he was created with love and intention.

After the service, Logan sat quietly, flipping through his Bible. He found the page he was looking for and began to read:

"You have searched me, Lord, and you know me. You know when I sit and when I rise; you perceive my thoughts from afar. You hem me in behind and before, and you lay your hand upon me."

The words washed over him, filling him with a sense of awe. How could it be that every part of him, even the parts he didn't like, were known by God? That the One who created the universe had taken the time to know him so deeply?

"I praise you because I am fearfully and wonderfully made; your works are wonderful, I know that full well."

Logan smiled to himself, feeling a warmth in his heart that he hadn't felt in a long time. He wasn't just a face in the crowd, not just another person trying to fit into the world's impossible standards. He was known, seen, and loved by the Creator of everything. And that was enough.

That afternoon, as Logan walked home, Ari walked quietly beside him.

"You're feeling better today," Ari observed, his voice gentle.

Logan nodded. "Yeah, I think I just needed to be reminded that I don't have to be perfect. That I'm enough as I am."

Ari smiled. "Exactly. Psalm 139 is a reminder that you are never forgotten, never overlooked. You are always known, always loved, no matter where you are or what you're going through."

Logan glanced up at the sky, feeling a lightness in his heart that had been missing for a while. "It's kind of amazing when you think about it. That God would care that much. That He would know every little thing about me and still… love me."

Ari's eyes twinkled. "It's more than amazing. It's the truth. And whenever you forget it, just remember that you are fearfully and wonderfully made—exactly as you are."

Logan smiled, feeling a sense of peace wash over him. No longer weighed down by the pressures of the world, he felt free. Free to be himself, free to live in the truth that he was known and loved by the One who made him.

And as he walked home, with Ari by his side, he knew that no matter where life took him, he would never be alone.

Reflection Questions:

1. When you feel like you're not enough, how can you remind yourself that you are "fearfully and wonderfully made"?

2. What makes you feel valuable? How can you learn to value yourself, even when the world around you makes you feel like you're not enough?

3. What parts of yourself do you hide because you think they aren't good enough? How can you start to embrace those parts as part of who you are?

4. How can knowing that you are deeply loved and known change the way you see yourself?

Quote:
"To be yourself in a world that is constantly trying to make you something else is the greatest accomplishment." – Ralph Waldo Emerson

Bible Verse:
"I praise you because I am fearfully and wonderfully made; your works are wonderful, I know that full well." – Psalm 139:14

You are loved.

Your potential is boundless.

CHAPTER 22

A Future and a Hope

The days had started blending together. School, home, friends—it all felt like one endless loop, and Logan couldn't shake the feeling that he was stuck. He didn't know what his future looked like, and that scared him.

Lately, everyone seemed to be talking about their plans. Some of his friends were already thinking about college, talking about what they wanted to major in, what their lives would look like in a few years. But Logan? He had no idea. The pressure to figure it all out weighed heavy on his chest. It felt like everyone else knew where they were going, and he was just… lost.

One afternoon, after another long day of feeling like he was drifting, Logan found himself sitting on the porch steps, staring out at the empty street. Ari, as usual, was quietly beside him, always present but never pushing.

"What's going on in your mind today?" Ari asked, his voice gentle, sensing the turmoil within Logan.

Logan sighed, resting his elbows on his knees. "I don't know. It feels like everyone knows what they want out of life, and I'm just… here. Stuck. Like, what if I never figure it out? What if I never find out what I'm supposed to do?"

Ari looked up at him, his golden eyes full of calm wisdom. "It's okay not to have all the answers right now, Logan. Life isn't about knowing every step in advance."

Logan rubbed his face with his hands, feeling the frustration bubbling up. "But it feels like I should have it figured out. Everyone else is talking about their plans—college, careers—and I don't even know what tomorrow looks like for me."

Ari was silent for a moment, then spoke softly. "Have you ever heard of Jeremiah 29:11?"

Logan paused, thinking. "Yeah… I think so. Isn't that the one about God's plans?"

Ari nodded. "It says, 'For I know the plans I have for you,' declares the Lord, 'plans to prosper you and not to harm you, plans to give you hope and a future.'"

Logan stared out at the street, letting the words sink in. "So, God has a plan for me? Even if I don't know what it is?"

"Exactly," Ari said, his voice filled with certainty. "Just because you don't know all the details doesn't mean the plan isn't there. God's timing is perfect, even when it doesn't align with your own. You're not supposed to have everything figured out right now. You're supposed to trust that there's a future full of hope, even when you can't see it."

Logan sat quietly, the weight of his uncertainty still heavy but beginning to shift. "But it's hard to trust that sometimes. What if I never figure it out? What if I'm not good enough to live up to that plan?"

Ari smiled softly. "God's plans for you don't depend on your perfection. They're rooted in His love and purpose for your life. He knows your strengths, your weaknesses, and your fears—and still, His plans are to give you hope and a future."

Later that evening, Logan found himself in his room, thinking about the conversation with Ari.

He grabbed his Bible and flipped through the pages until he found the verse Ari had mentioned. Jeremiah 29:11.

"'For I know the plans I have for you,' declares the Lord, 'plans to prosper you and not to harm you, plans to give you hope and a future.'"

Logan read the words over and over again, trying to make sense of them in his own life. The truth was, he had been feeling lost for a long time. He wasn't sure what direction he wanted to take. But this verse? It felt like a promise. A reminder that even though he didn't know what the future held, someone did. And that someone had a plan for him—one that was good, one that gave him hope.

The next day at school, the pressure returned.

Everyone was buzzing about college applications and future plans. Logan's friends were talking about their dream schools, their goals, and the paths they wanted to take. Logan, meanwhile, felt the familiar wave of doubt wash over him.

Daniel, noticing Logan's silence, nudged him. "You alright? You've been pretty quiet lately."

Logan shrugged. "Yeah, just… thinking about the future. It feels like everyone has their plan except me."

Daniel nodded. "Yeah, it's stressful. But you don't have to have it all figured out right now. We're only teenagers, man."

Logan laughed a little, appreciating the reminder. "True. I guess I just keep thinking that I should know more by now."

Daniel raised an eyebrow. "Since when do you need to have your whole life mapped out? You'll figure it out as you go. No rush."

Logan smiled, feeling a bit of relief. He was beginning to understand that maybe he didn't need to have everything planned out just yet. Maybe there was something bigger at work—something he couldn't see, but could trust in.

As the day went on, Logan kept thinking about Jeremiah 29:11. The words echoed in his mind, a promise that he could lean on during times of uncertainty. He might not know every step of his future, but he could trust that there was a plan for him, and that plan was filled with hope.

That evening, as Logan sat with Ari under the stars, he felt a new sense of peace.

"I've been thinking a lot about that verse," Logan said, looking over at Ari.

"About how God knows the plans He has for me, even when I don't."

Ari smiled, his eyes reflecting the light of the stars. "It's a comforting thought, isn't it? Knowing that you don't have to carry the weight of your future alone. There's a path already laid out for you, even if you can't see it yet."

Logan nodded, feeling the tension in his chest slowly easing. "Yeah. I think I'm starting to understand that it's okay not to know everything. That maybe part of trusting God's plan is being okay with the uncertainty."

Ari's tail flicked softly. "Exactly. Trust is about letting go of the need to control everything and believing that the One who created you knows exactly where you're going, even when the road looks unclear."

Logan looked up at the stars, feeling a deep sense of gratitude. He still didn't know what his future looked like, but for the first time, he didn't feel afraid of the unknown. He knew that he wasn't walking the path alone, and that gave him the strength to move forward, one step at a time.

And as he sat under the vast sky, Logan whispered the words of Jeremiah 29:11 to himself, holding onto the promise of hope and a future.

Reflection Questions:

1. Do you feel pressure to have your future figured out? How does that pressure affect you?

2. How can you learn to trust that there is a plan for your life, even when you don't know all the details yet?

3. What can you do to ease the anxiety of not knowing what the future holds? Who or what can help you feel more at peace?

4. How do you define "hope" in your own life? What does it mean to you to have hope for the future, even when it feels uncertain?

Quote:
"Trust the wait. Embrace the uncertainty. Enjoy the beauty of becoming. When nothing is certain, anything is possible." – Mandy Hale

Bible Verse:
"For I know the plans I have for you," declares the Lord, "plans to prosper you and not to harm you, plans to give you hope and a future." – Jeremiah 29:11

Conclusion

Life can feel overwhelming sometimes, especially when you're trying to figure out who you are and where you belong. There are moments when the weight of expectations, the fear of not being enough, or the uncertainty of the future feels like too much to carry.

For Logan, those moments were real. But so was Ari.

Ari wasn't just any lion. He wasn't the kind you'd find in a zoo or read about in a textbook. He was something deeper—something quiet yet powerful. He didn't roar for attention, and he never forced his way in. Instead, he was simply there—whenever Logan needed him most.

At first, it seemed like Ari belonged only to Logan. He was invisible to others, a private source of courage, a voice that whispered strength when the world felt too loud. But as time went on, something became clear: Ari wasn't just Logan's. Somehow, in ways that weren't always easy to explain, he showed up for others too—Daniel, Emma, and maybe even you.

Maybe that's because we all have an Ari in our lives. Maybe he isn't a lion, but a trusted friend, a mentor, a parent, or even our faith. Maybe he's that gentle, steady voice inside us that reminds us we are stronger than we think, braver than we feel, and never as alone as we fear.

Ari never came to take Logan's struggles away. He came to remind Logan that he was never facing them alone. And that's what I want you to know too.

You don't have to have everything figured out right now. It's okay to feel lost, to wonder if you're enough, to struggle with the big questions of life. But please remember this: everything you need to get through your hardest days is already inside you.

You are stronger than you know.
You are braver than you feel.
You are loved more than you realize.

The road ahead might not always be easy, but you don't have to walk it alone. The strength you need may not roar like a lion, but it is there, walking beside you, whispering when you need it most.

And if you ever forget, I hope you remember Ari.

Because if nothing else, let this be your reminder:

You are seen. You are valued. You belong.
Keep going. The best parts of your story are still being written.

To the "Lion" that leads you,

Maria Gregory

About The Author

Maria Gregory is a natural storyteller and visionary, whose heart beats at the core of The Lion You Don't See. As the founder of the I RiseUp Group of Companies—which includes I Riseup Academy, I Riseup Foundation, and CLICK - Computer Learning for Inner City Kids—Maria is on a mission to empower people to find their inner strength and realize the incredible possibilities that life has to offer.

Maria's journey has been one of service and growth. With a background deeply rooted in both counseling and education, she proudly served as a Presidential Member of the American Christian Counselors Association from 2009 to 2020, offering guidance and support to countless individuals as they navigated their own paths of healing and personal growth. She also spent over a decade as a volunteer Big Sister with Big Brothers Big Sisters of America (BBBS) from 2004 to 2016, mentoring young people and encouraging them to reach for their full potential.

From 2012 to 2014, and 2018, Maria also served as a Judge for the Invention Convention League, where she helped inspire the next generation of inventors and creators. But Maria's dedication to making a difference doesn't stop at her professional life. She wears many hats—wife, stepmom, big sister, aunt, godmother, and trusted friend you can rely on—finding joy in nurturing the people she's called to serve and support. Her passion for community and personal connection fuels everything she does.

The Lion You Don't See is a project that's especially close to Maria's heart. Inspired by her own desire to help readers of all ages uncover the quiet, often hidden strength inside them, she believes that through the power of storytelling, people can begin to see beyond their struggles and recognize the courage they didn't even know they had.

Maria's ultimate goal? To show you that the lion you don't see is roaring inside you, just waiting to be discovered.